# CREATIVITY AND CONFORMITY

CLARK E. MOUSTAKAS
*The Merrill-Palmer Institute*



AN INSIGHT BOOK

D. VAN NOSTRAND COMPANY
NEW YORK, CINCINNATI
TORONTO LONDON MELBOURNE

D. Van Nostrand Company Regional Offices:
*New York Cincinnati Millbrae*

D. Van Nostrand Reinhold Company International Offices:
*London Toronto Melbourne*



Published by D. Van Nostrand Company
450 West 33rd Street, New York, N.Y. 10001

Published simultaneously in Canada by
Van Nostrand Reinhold Ltd.

12 11 10 9 8

For Beth
Steve
Kerry
Wendy
who, in daily encounters,
keep alive the essence and
spirit of creative life.

# Foreword

This book takes a stand in behalf of individuality and creativity and discusses the consequences of widespread conformity in modern life. An effort is made to evolve a meaningful understanding of creativity, self-growth, and self-renewal and to show that significant strides in knowledge and awareness are essentially the reflection of a light which is kindled from within the self and not from external sources.

Human ethics and ideals, concepts and values, are explored and illustrated as a way of revealing the interior regions of man, the underlying dimensions of genuine life which are being threatened and destroyed by a society which has increasingly extended materialistic incentives and accomplishments but which has failed to keep touch with the aesthetic side of man, with the mystery and wonder in the universe with ethical and moral value; a society which has expanded its resources for bodily satisfactions and pleasures but which has not kept pace in the realm of spirit; a society which has improved physical health and increased the life span but which has not enabled creation of meanings and roots which sustain and enhance the well-being of the individual as a whole person.

An examination is made of methods and procedures which diagnose, analyze and evaluate the person, and break him up for study in such a way that nothing at all is left of the person as a substantial reality. Real understanding of the individual does not come from viewing the person as an object for analysis and study, from noting his behavior and probing into the so-called hidden dynamics, frustrations, and conflicts of his past life. Genuine understanding is not a shrewd analysis which is disclosed by strange signs and symbols, not a clever diagnosis which has a keen eye for the weaknesses of people but rather it is rooted in life itself, in living with the other person, in being sensitive and aware of the center of a person's world, perceiving the essential nature of the person as he is, and respecting and valuing his resources and strengths. Only when the person is recognized as an integrated being with self-determining resources is there hope that a unity of mankind can also be born.

Two ways are explored—the confrontation and the encounter—in which man in his relationship to man breaks through the steady monotony of routine habits and patterns of conventional living, through which man dispenses with social and professional roles and speaks as a whole person, openly and honestly. In a time when genuine involvement and commitment are rare, when people are afraid to face each other in the real issues which exist between them, afraid to challenge and threaten the stability and security of their lives, the confrontation takes on an added significance. In this book, the confrontation is viewed as a creative struggle between persons who are engaged in a dispute or controversy and who remain together, face to face, until acceptance, respect for differences, and love emerge; even though the persons may be at odds in terms of the issue they are no longer at odds with each other.

In contrast, the encounter is a meeting of harmony and mutuality, a feeling of being within the life of another person while at the same time maintaining one's own identity and individuality. The encounter is a decisive inner experience in which new dimensions of the self are revealed (not as intellectual knowledge but as integral awareness) and broadening and enlarging values in communal life are discovered.

The book also discusses the relationship between honesty and the well-being of the person. Honesty of self is seen as the quality which unifies the self and provides the active moral sense which governs one's actions. When we are not honest, we are not all there. That part of us which if expressed would make us whole is buried, and a false, distorted image replaces the real self. At first the individual is aware of the distortions between the real self and his stated thoughts and feelings, but, with repeated experience, self-awareness slips into self-deception and the individual no longer knows what is fantasy and what is reality. There is an additional tragedy: others are taken in by the lie and the dishonesty spreads and leads to profound and inevitable anguish and destruction.

Today the powers and resources of official society are used to promote conceptions of the good life which center in status, economic security, intellectual accomplishments, and materialistic gains. Self-protection, maintenance of a stable life, conformity and socialization are the primary goals. A counter position is needed to advance the value of utilizing human potentialities in the development of unique individuals growing toward creative selfhood. This does not mean that creativity and individuality are ideals in contrast to the evils of convention and conformity but rather it means that modern man is so surrounded and pressed to strive for standards and goals that contradict his own growing selfhood that he needs the opposite confirming stand of individuality and uniqueness, the affirmation of self-values that encourage and enhance creative life, to combat the powerful forces in society which tend to squelch deviation and difference.

Modern man must keep a focus on his search for identity and on the value of authentic life; he must remain sensitive to his own inner experience and to the human dimensions in the world; he must continue to feel the suffering and grief which surround him and be awakened by the brutality and tragedy as well as by the joy and happiness which exist in the world.

Both creativity and materialism are aspects of being human but they are no longer in harmony, no longer in balance as values in modern society. We must not be bounded by any system, whether social or intellectual, but by a moral strength which can be exercised in real moments of life with other persons; we must not be guided by rules and instructions but by ethical value which remains in the deep regions of the self and provides a direction for meeting the requirements of each situation as it is lived. Education and socialization must not only help the individual to become more skillful, more informed, more secure, and more socially effective, but it must also enable the person to evolve a unique self, to actualize his particular talents, and to engender an authenticity and substance in life that will have enduring value. Society must encourage and help the person to evolve a life that is not only enlightened and informed but also honest, just, beautiful, whole, courageous, and good.

The chapters as they now stand (although revised so that they are consistent with my current thinking and experience) are based on previously published articles, papers presented at conferences and workshops, lectures to seminar groups, and notes taken during periods of self-reflection and study over the past ten years. Each article had its beginning under widely different circumstances and conditions. Each was related in some way to my own experience—critical incidents, challenging questions and problems, issues, encounters—in which I was stuck as an individual, or challenged in such a way that only by searching into my own thought and feeling could I begin to move forward to new awareness and new direction. The written form was my way of inquiring into a theme that was central to my growth as a professional person and as a private individual, my way of seeking to come to terms with the world on a creative basis when life was being threatened by pretense and distortion, by rules and routines, and by meaningless standards and conventions.

Although these essays are related in theme, each was created at a different time and place and presented to diverse audiences. A continuous reading experience may be the best approach for some readers, but I believe that intervals of time should be left between each chapter for study and reflection. The papers, more or less, fall into two general groupings. The first is concerned with creativity and conformity, individuality and uniqueness, and man's relationship to man. The second focusses on ethical and moral value and man's search for enduring truth and meaning in a world where life can be easily shattered, in a society threatened by dehumanization and by moral bankruptcy.

CLARK E. MOUSTAKAS

# Acknowledgments

Many persons, both directly and indirectly, helped to make this book a reality.

First, I wish to acknowledge my appreciation to the following individuals who in their own hours of creativity and conformity contributed essays, letters, and poems which I have used as illustrations in the book: Eve Winn, Eugene Alexander, Paul Jensen, Janet Petersen, Nancy Dee, and David Harris.

Second, I express my thanks to my graduate students enrolled in my courses Personal Growth and Psychological Counseling, and Psychotherapy with Children at The Merrill-Palmer Institute, and to the students who have registered in my Human Relations Seminars in the Lincoln Park Public Schools, the Plymouth Public Schools, and the Royal Oak Public Schools, who gave me the opportunity over the past ten years to explore my thinking and experience in a receptive and valuing atmosphere.

Third, my development as a professional person and as an individual with reference to the themes of this book have been enhanced by the following persons, in direct confrontations and encounters, or through their published works: Dorothy Lee, A. H. Maslow, Carl Rogers, David Smillie, Ross Mooney, Martin Buber, Laurens Van der Post, Witter Bynner, Viktor E. Frankl, and Kahlil Gibran.

Fourth, the study was made possible by the encouragement and support of Pauline P. W. Knapp, President of The Merrill-Palmer Institute, where freedom and individuality are still valued in education; Melvyn Baer, who provided the essential directedness in proofreading; Julie Mills and Dora Dawson, who assisted with manuscript correction; Roseanne Ellicott and Mavis Wolfe, who typed the original manuscript, putting almost illegible notes into readable form; and my wife, Betty, who was genuinely present throughout and enabled the creative process.

Fifth, I express my appreciation to the following authors and publishers for permission to reprint excerpts from their works, listed in the order in which they appear in the chapters of this book:

1. Uniqueness and Individuality:

MAY, ROLLO. *Man's Search for Himself*. Copyright 1953 by W. W. Norton and Company.

2. The Sense of Self:

BUCKE, RICHARD M. *Cosmic Consciousness*. Copyright 1901 by E. P. Dutton and Company, Inc.

BYNNER, WITTER. *THE WAY OF LIFE: According to Laotzu*. Copyright 1944 by Witter Bynner. The John Day Company, Inc., Publisher.

GUÉRARD, ALBERT. *Bottle in the Sea*. Copyright 1954 by Harvard University Press.

MOUSTAKAS, CLARK E. The Sense of Self. *Journal of Humanistic Psychology*, Vol. 1, No. 1, Spring 1961.

PATTON, KENNETH L. *Man's Hidden Search*. Copyright 1954 by Meeting House Press.

VAN DER POST, LAURENS. *Venture to the Interior*. Copyright 1951 by Laurens Van der Post. William Morrow and Co., Inc. and The Hogarth Press, Ltd., Publishers.

3. Creativity and Conformity:

BUBER, MARTIN. *Hasidism and Modern Man*. Edited and translated by Maurice Friedman. Copyright 1958 by Horizon Press.

BYNNER, WITTER. *THE WAY OF LIFE: According to Laotzu*. Copyright 1944 by Witter Bynner. The John Day Company, Inc., Publisher.

HORNEY, KAREN. Finding the Real Self. *American Journal of Psychoanalysis*. Vol. 9, 1949.

KELMAN, HAROLD. Communing and Relating: Part III —Examples: General and Clinical. *American Journal of Psychoanalysis*. Vol. 19, 1959.

MOUSTAKAS, CLARK E. Creativity, Conformity, and The Self, in *Creativity and Psychological Health*. Edited by Michael Andrews. Copyright 1961 by Syracuse University Press.

MOUSTAKAS, CLARK E. *Psychotherapy with Children.* Copyright 1959 by Clark E. Moustakas. Harper and Row, Publishers.

REIK, THEODORE. *The Search Within.* Copyright 1956 by Farrar, Strauss and Giroux, Incorporated.

WILL, OTTO A. and COHEN, ROBERT A. A Report of a Recorded Interview in the Course of Psychotherapy. *Psychiatry.* Vol. 16, 1953. Copyright by William Alanson White Psychiatric Foundation.

4. Confrontation and Encounter:

BUBER, MARTIN. *Between Man and Man.* Translated by Ronald G. Smith. Copyright 1947 by Routledge and Kegan Paul Ltd.

BUBER, MARTIN. *Hasidism and Modern Man.* Edited and translated by Maurice Friedman. Copyright 1958 by Horizon Press.

COUSINS, NORMAN. The Desensitization of Twentieth-Century Man. *Saturday Review.* May 16, 1959.

FRANKL, VIKTOR E. *Man's Search for Meaning: An Introduction to Logotherapy.* Copyright 1962 by Beacon Press and by Hodder and Stoughton.

MOUSTAKAS, CLARK E. Confrontation and Encounter. *Journal of Existentialism.* Vol. 2, No. 7, Winter 1962.

MOUSTAKAS, CLARK E. *Loneliness.* Copyright 1961 by Clark E. Moustakas. Prentice-Hall Incorporated, Publishers.

MOUSTAKAS, CLARK E. *Psychotherapy With Children.* Copyright 1959 by Clark E. Moustakas. Harper and Row, Publishers.

5. Honesty, Idiocy and Manipulation:

BUBER, MARTIN. *Between Man and Man.* Translated by Ronald C. Smith. Copyright 1947 by Routledge and Kegan Paul Ltd.

BUBER, MARTIN. *Hasidism and Modern Man.* Edited and translated by Maurice Friedman. Copyright 1958 by Horizon Press.

DOSTOEVSKI, FYODOR. *The Idiot.* Copyright 1958 by Bantam Books, Inc.

EWALD, CARL. *My Little Boy*. Copyright 1906 by Charles Scribner's Sons.

MOUSTAKAS, CLARK E. Honesty, Idiocy, and Manipulation. *Journal of Humanistic Psychology*. Vol. 2, No. 2, Fall 1962.

OSBORNE, REBECCA M. The Mental Patient and the Sense of Conspiracy. *Inward Light*. Vol. 33, Fall 1960.

SHLIEN, JOHN. The Client-Centered Approach to Schizophrenia: A First Approximation. *Psychotherapy of the Psychoses*. Edited by Arthur Burton. Copyright 1960 by Basic Books.

6. Beyond Good and Evil:

BERKELEY, GEORGE. *The Principles of Human Knowledge*. Copyright 1963 by World Publishing Company.

BUBER, MARTIN. *Good and Evil*. Translated by Ronald G. Smith. Copyright 1952 by Charles Scribner's Sons.

MOORE, GEORGE E. *Principia Ethica*. Copyright 1903 by Cambridge University Press.

NIETZCHE, FRIEDRICH. *Beyond Good and Evil*. Translated by Marianne Cowan. Copyright 1955 by Henry Regnery Company.

PLATO. *The Republic*. Translated by B. Jowett. Copyright by Oxford University Press, Inc. A Vintage Book published by Random House 1961.

7. Ethical and Moral Value:

BUBER, MARTIN. *Between Man and Man*. Translated by Ronald G. Smith. Copyright 1947 by Routledge and Kegan Paul Ltd.

MOORE, GEORGE E. *Principia Ethica*. Copyright 1903 by Cambridge University Press.

YEVTUSHENKO, YEVGENY. *A Precocious Autobiography*. Translated by Andrew R. MacAndrew. Copyright 1963 by E. P. Dutton & Co. Inc.

8. Self-Doubt and Self-Inquiry:

DOSTOEVSKI, FYODOR. *Notes from Underground and the Grand Inquisitor*. Translated by Ralph Matlaw. Copyright 1960 by E. P. Dutton and Company, Incorporated. Dutton Paperback Series.

MACLEISH, ARCHIBALD. *J.B.* R.C.A. Records. Elia Kazan Producer.

TOLSTOI, LEO. Family Happiness in *The Death of Ivan Ilych and Other Stories.* Copyright 1960 by Oxford University Press, Incorporated.

TOLSTOI, LEO. The Death of Ivan Ilych in *Quintet.* Copyright 1956 by Pyramid Books.

9. Dimensions of the Creative Life:

KIERKEGAARD, SØREN. *A Kierkegaard Anthology.* Edited by Robert Bretall. Copyright 1951 by Princeton University Press.

MOUSTAKAS, CLARK E. (Editor) *The Self: Explorations in Personal Growth.* Copyright 1956 by Clark E. Moustakas. Harper and Row, Publishers.

PROGOFF, IRA. *The Symbolic and The Real.* Copyright 1963 by Julian Press Incorporated.

RILKE, RAINER MARIA. *Letters to a Young Poet.* Translated by M. D. Herter Norton. Copyright 1934 by W. W. Norton and Company Incorporated. Renewed 1962 by M. D. Herter Norton. Revised Edition Copyright 1954 by W. W. Norton and Company, Incorporated.

STEINBECK, JOHN and RICKETTS, EDWARD F. *Sea of Cortez.* Copyright 1941 by Viking Press Incorporated.

C.E.M.

# Contents

# CREATIVITY AND CONFORMITY

# I

## Uniqueness and Individuality

Experience is true to the person when he is himself alone—and not any other person or thing. Every individual embodies and contains a uniqueness, a reality, that makes him unlike any other person or thing. To maintain this uniqueness in the face of threats and pressures, in times of shifting patterns and moods, is the ultimate challenge and responsibility of every man. In true experience, perception is unique and undifferentiated; there is a sense of wholeness, unity, and centeredness. In such moments, man is immersed in the world, exploring, spontaneously expressing himself, and finding satisfaction in being rooted to life as a whole person.

When man is intimately related to life, he neither ties himself to restricted goals that he must pursue; nor is he confined by directions and instructions and rules, or restrained by patterned or conditioned responses and techniques. He is free; he is open; he is direct; he encounters life with all of his resources; and he lives in accordance with the unique requirements of each situation as it unfolds before him. Neither bound by the past, nor fixed to the present, the creative man can transcend the limits of history and time by realizing new facets of himself and by relating to the demands of existence in new ways. The reality of one's own personal experience may be understood through self-reflection, in times of loneliness or isolation, and in moments of communal life.

Experience is real only when it is being lived; as soon as it is talked about or defined, the living moment is lost. Efforts to communicate the real self inevitably distort its reality and violate the integral nature of life. To define the self we must categorize, compare, and describe. We must treat the person as a list of traits; and, in the process, the living substance of the unique individual is destroyed. Attempts to communicate the self at best touch upon surface features, but the real self remains unrecognized and unknown. The real self can never be known through diagnosis, analysis, and evaluation; these methods destroy its wholeness and leave only bits and pieces.

The self is itself alone, existing as a whole, with enduring presence and emerging patterns. Because of its complexity and depth, the self cannot be fully known; but its qualities or states can be felt and perceived as reflections of an inconceivable totality or whole. The self may stand out in bold relief, or it may blend imperceptibly with other forms in nature and in the universe.

Healthy communal life can be established only in a setting where the person is free to explore his capacities and to discover for himself meanings and values that will enable him to create an identity. We can help a person to be himself by our own willingness to steep ourselves temporarily in his world, in his private feelings and experiences. By our affirmation of the person as he is, we give him support and strength to take the next step in his own growth.

As long as a person maintains the integrity and uniqueness of his individual nature, growth of the self (which begins at birth) continues throughout life. The urge to express one's individual nature and come to full self-realization lies within each person. It is neither a quiescent drive that must be activated by external pressures and motivations nor an effort to relieve tensions. On the contrary, the urge to become is a positive force.

Only the individual can actualize his potentialities. He must do his own learning and he must do his own growing. The self by its nature is inclined to grow and moves toward an evolving identity and an individuality that has an irrevocable biological basis. Although tissues continually change, individual specificity persists during the entire life; although organs of the body move toward definitive transformations and death, they always maintain their unique qualities (6, p. 267). Inherent in every higher organism is something that differentiates one individual from every other individual, a difference that can be discovered by observing the reactions of certain cells and tissues belonging to one individual in contrast to the tissues and cells of another individual of the same species (14, p. 4). To the extent that the intrinsic nature of the individual is nourished and cultivated, the person maintains his integrity, and moves toward originality of expression and actualization of his potentialities.

Often a person is known in terms of his "what-ness" rather than his "who-ness"—in terms of what he represents and what he can do rather than who he is. Evaluating a person from his products reveals only a fragmented picture of where he has been, but not who he is or where he is going. Potential and promise are more clearly disclosed in a man's desire for experience and his thirst for knowledge than in records, scores, and grades.

In spite of all the advances in personality tests and measures for analyzing human behavior, understanding the person from his own point of view, in the light of his own unique experiences, desires, and interests, is still the most real way of knowing him. To see the person as he sees himself is a way of respecting him, of sharing his dreams and yearnings, his fears and hopes, his optimism and disillusion, his perceptions of himself and the world.

The growing evidence that most people can state their experiences honestly and directly has not caused us to feel any more trusting of self reports. We still have not grasped the notion that, in most instances, a straight question will get a straight answer. The tendency remains to rely heavily on external measures. The widespread use of lie detector machines, projective tests, and similar devices attests to this distrust of man.

The absurdity of relying on mechanical tests and devices rather than on men themselves was pointed up in a series of motivation studies. In these studies, the projective tests failed to reveal the craving for food among men on a starvation diet (2). The number of food associations actually declined with longer periods of fasting. No one would question the importance of extreme hunger in motivating behavior yet this motive was not uncovered by mechanical devices. It was, however, easily disclosed in conversation with the men.

We can know the meanings experiences have for others by listening with objectivity and attempting to understand the essence of the experience through the person's relating it. Objectivity here refers to seeing what an experience *is* for another person, not how it fits or relates to other experiences—not what causes it, why it exists, or what purpose it serves. It is an attempt to see attitudes and concepts, beliefs and values of an individual as they are to him at the moment he expresses them—not what they were or will become. The experience of the other person as he perceives it is sufficient unto itself, and can be understood in terms of itself alone.

Knowing only the content of an experience does not convey its unique meaning any more than knowing that a tree has a trunk and branches tells how it will be perceived by the different people who see it. The "facts" regarding human behavior have little meaning in themselves. It is the manner in which they are perceived and known that reveals how they will be expressed in behavior. Experiments at the Hanover Institute have shown that we do not receive our perceptions from the things around us, but rather that our perceptions come from within us (12). There is no reality except individual reality and that is based on a background of unique experience.

Complex and thorough examination sometimes is required to diagnose tuberculosis, cancer, or a heart ailment; but knowing about the presence of a serious illness does not tell what it will mean in the life of the sick person or his family. A group of physicians may find it easy to communicate with each other regarding the nature of an illness, but difficult to talk to the patient when they have not taken into account the patient's perceptions of his illness. When the physician doubts the impact of the patient's self-perception of his illness, he distrusts the potential curative powers within the person and his striving for health. This reduces his resources for recovery and weakens his self-confidence. To the extent that physicians fail to consider the patient's private experience, they do not understand the full nature of the illness. If they show complete confidence in the medical aspects of the patient but little recognition of him as a unique, special individual, they miss a critical dimension of the illness—the fact that each person is unlike any other who has had a painful disease.

When experts fail to recognize that facts attain meaning in a personal context and that the meaning differs for each person, then they fail to understand fully the true nature of a fact. Generalizations about human growth and development do not apply to the particular person, and recommendations based on "facts" without reference to personal experience often cannot be accepted and utilized by him. Rather than having a constructive value in meeting problems in living, such recommendations frighten and immobilize the person and prolong the solution of the problem.

Analytic people tend to see an individual in terms of someone else—his father, his mother, his siblings, thus distorting his real nature. One does not recognize the otherness of a person by projecting onto him someone else or by abstracting out of him transferred feelings and attitudes. When one sees in a person his father or mother or anyone else, one ignores the person as he really is. This conveys a fundamental disregard for and a destructive attitude toward the person. Real understanding is not some shrewd analysis that has a keen eye for people's weaknesses, but a deep perception of the core, of the essential nature of the other person (3). In the final analysis the individual must know for himself the totality that he is. The ultimate meaning of a person's life depends on the values and convictions he has developed and only the individual himself can convey this meaning.

All psychological phenomena can be understood as illustrating the single principle of unity or self-consistency (13). When the individual becomes a real person there is not only integrity and unity in his experience, but also fullness and variety. Harmony in life comes from an increasing capacity to find in the world that which also obtains within the depths of one's own being (18).

Resistance to external pressure permits a person to maintain self-consistency. It is a healthy response, indicating that the will of the individual is still intact. It is the person's effort to sustain his integrity. When he submits to external demands and threats, he is weakened and unable to function effectively as a self. A man will resist the attempts to change him that threaten his perception of himself and will respond to situations that permit him to express and explore his potentials. He will not respond to stimuli that do not fit his own sense of self. Such stimuli can be effective only if they are very strong and force themselves upon him. Then he is driven into a catastrophic situation, not only because he is unable to express himself in a healthy way but also because he is shocked and disturbed—sometimes so severely he is unable to react at all (10). Similarly, when we force a person to behave according to our own values, when we impose our convictions on him, we impair his creativity and his will to explore and actualize.

Otto Rank (20) stressed the importance of positive will expression. He believed that its denial is the essence of neurosis. His aim was to strengthen will, not weaken it. Confronted by external pressures (attempts to frighten and even terrify the person, to force him to submit to symbols, standards, and values outside himself), a person must often call upon forces from within himself, follow his internal cues, and assert himself in order to retain his identity. If he does conform while the core of his being cries out against conformity, his health and stability are jeopardized and he is often unable to think, decide, or act. Sometimes he assumes the expectations, convictions, and values of others, ceasing to be a real self and wearing the masks of convention and propriety.

Expressions of the real self reflect the natural emergence of potentiality. They are unified and consistent in behavior, not the wild, confused and fragmentary "acting out" often designated as self-expression. This kind of self-expression is a reaction to frustration, denial, and rejection, to not being a self. An expression of the self must recognize personal individuality and be a source for the realization of goodness in others. As Reinhold Niebuhr has stated: "There is no point at which the self, seeking its own, can feel itself self-satisfied and free to consider others than itself. The concern for others is as immediate as the concern for itself" (19, p. 139). Respect for one's own integrity and uniqueness, love for and understanding of one's own self, cannot be separated from the respect, love, and understanding of another person (9). The creative expression of the self is always constructive (20). The following quotation (17, p. 56) shows how misunderstanding and confusion arise when the nature of self-expression is distorted:

> Those of us who lived in the 1920's can recall the evidences of the growing tendency to think of the self in superficial and oversimplified terms. In those days "self-expression" was supposed to be simply doing whatever popped into one's head, as though the self were synonymous with any random impulse, and as though one's decision were to be made on the basis of a whim which might be a product of digestion from a hurried lunch just as often as one's philosophy of life. To "be yourself" was then an excuse to relaxing into the lowest common denominator of inclination. To "know one's self" wasn't thought to be especially different and the problems of personality could be resolved relatively easily by better "adjustment."

If real expression of the self can be a bad thing, the blame lies not with it but with providence (8). Unless the person is free to express his own uniqueness and distinctiveness, his capacity for growth is stifled and denied. Self-expression is the individual's way of asserting his own yes-feeling.

Desire is not a blind and capricious impulse but a necessary urge that makes vital experience possible. It is actively surging forward to break through whatever dams it up (8). To desire is to want, to feel, to be free to choose. The person must know what he wants, though not necessarily in a conscious, deliberate way. Knowing what one wants is simply the elemental ability to choose one's own values (17).

As long as a situation has a genuine appeal to a person, it is not necessary to ask what it is good for. As John Dewey has indicated (7, p. 283), "This is a question which can be asked only about instrumental values, but some goods are not *good* for anything; they are just goods. Any other notion leads to an absurdity."

When we reject the desires and interests of another person, we are also rejecting him. Because the self exists as a whole, rejection of significant dimensions of the self are experienced by a person as the rejection of the entire self, even though the criticizer or rejecter believes he is separating the individual from his behavior and condemning only the behavior. The expression, "I love you but not what you do," implies that a person exists in parts. Even if a person feels loving while rejecting the actions of another individual (and this is probably rare), the rejecter is split, with part of him confirming and part of him condemning the other.

Rejection of another person through a rejection of his behavior is tempered when we sympathize with him, when we understand and appreciate his feelings and wishes. If we usually accept and value the person, the bonds established by the positive moments will sustain us in the rejecting moments. It takes courage to recognize and admit rejecting feelings for those whom we ordinarily cherish, but if the rejection is occasional, the feeling of love will endure in the relationship. The struggle between persons is always away from fragmentation of the self into categories, and toward a unification of persons as whole beings. Thus temporary rejection implies upheaval and conflict; the persons involved in the conflict, although basically accepting each other, seek a new pattern of relationship and a new level of unity.

Rejection often occurs because we fear that if we permit an individual to explore his desires and interests in his own way he will develop anti-social tendencies or become lazy and indifferent. We feel we have to condition him, teach him directly, keep after him to socialize him, to make him behave like others and become a responsible person. Nor do we trust ourselves or have confidence that our own personal experiences with the other person will provide a healthy basis for social growth.

Somehow we must remove the beliefs that make men mistrust themselves and each other. Having the freedom to grow and to actualize one's self provides the best foundation for interacting with others within groups, and in society. One cannot grow according to one's own nature unless he is free—and to be free is to accept oneself in totality, to respect one's individuality, and to be open and ready to engage in new experience. Freedom also means selecting those human values that will foster growth. John Dewey states that freedom contains three important elements: (1) efficiency in action and the absence of cramping and thwarting obstacles, (2) capacity to change the course of action and to experience novelties, and (3) the power of desire and choice to be factors in events (8). Freedom includes a basic attitude of allowing one's self to be the guiding force in significant experience, allowing one's self to discover truth and to express truth as one sees it.

There can be no freedom without responsibility, but self-discipline and self-responsibility are inherent tendencies in man (4). To be positively free is to be simultaneously spontaneous and thoughtful, self-enhancing and other-enhancing, self-valuing and valuing of others. When men are free to be themselves they do not violate the trust conveyed to them. When individual integrity is maintained and fostered society is enriched.

We must not accept as intrinsic the antagonism between individual interests and social interests. A. H. Maslow (15) has strongly emphasized that this kind of antagonism exists only in a sick society. Individual and social interests being synergetic, *not* antagonistic, creative individual expression results in social creativity and growth—which in turn encourage and free the individual to further self-expression and discovery. Individuality must be encouraged, not stifled. Only what is true and of value to society can emerge from genuine self-interest.

All people need love, safety, belongingness, acceptance, and respect as conditions basic to their growth. When these conditions are provided by the human environment, growth occurs naturally through actualization of one's potentials. We may offer resources, make available opportunities, and give information and help when it is needed. But to force standards, social values, and concepts on another person is to stifle his potential creativity and difference. Relations must be such that the individual is free to affirm, express, actualize, and experience his own uniqueness. We make this possible when we show that we deeply care for the other person, respect his individuality, and accept him without qualification.

To permit another person to be and become does not promote selfishness on his part. Rather it affirms his truly human self.

The following principles summarize a basic approach to the recognition of uniqueness and individuality:

1. The individual knows himself better than anyone else.
2. Only the individual can develop his potentialities.
3. The individual's perception of his own feelings, attitudes, and ideas is more valid than any outside diagnosis can be.
4. The individual, to keep on growing as a self, must continue to believe in himself, regardless of what anyone else may think of him. The belief in one's own reality is a necessary condition to the fulfillment of that reality.
5. Objects have no meaning in themselves. Individuals give meanings and reality to them. These meanings reflect the individual's background of experience.
6. Every individual is consistent and logical in the context of his own personal experience. He may seem inconsistent and illogical to others when he is not understood.
7. As long as the individual accepts and values himself, he will continue to grow and develop his potentialities. When he does not accept and value himself, much of his energies will be used to defend rather than to explore and to actualize himself.
8. Every individual wants to grow toward self-fulfillment. These growth strivings are present at all times.
9. An individual learns significantly only those things which are involved in the maintenance or enhancement of self. No one can force the individual to learn. He will learn only if he wills to. Any other type of learning is temporary and inconsistent with the self and will disappear as soon as threat is removed.
10. We cannot teach another person directly. We can make real learning possible by providing information, the setting, atmosphere, materials, resources, and by being there. The learning process itself is a unique, individualistic experience.
11. Under threat, the self is less open to spontaneous expression—that is, more passive and controlled. When

free from threat the self is more open—that is, free to be and free to strive toward actualization.

12. The situation which most effectively promotes significant learning is one in which (a) the threat to the self is at a minimum while at the same time the uniqueness of the individual is regarded as worthwhile and is deeply respected; and (b) the person is free to explore the materials and resources available to him and to select his own experiences in the light of his interests, desires, and potentialities.

## REFERENCES

1. ADLER, ALFRED. *Understanding Human Nature.* New York: Greenberg Publishers, Inc., 1927.
2. ALLPORT, GORDON W. The Trend in Motivational Theory. *Am. J. Orthopsychiatry,* 23:107-119(1953).
3. ANGYAL, ANDRAS. A Theoretical Model for Personality Studies. *J. Personality,* 20:131-141 (1951).
4. BRETALL, ROBERT (ed.). *A Kierkegaard Anthology.* Princeton: Princeton University Press, 1946.
5. BUBER, MARTIN. *Between Man and Man.* Tr. by Ronald Gregor Smith. Boston: Beacon Press, 1955.
6. CARREL, ALEXES. *Man the Unknown.* New York: Harper and Bros., 1935.
7. DEWEY, JOHN. *Democracy and Education.* New York: The MacMillan Co., 1916.
8. DEWEY, JOHN. *Human Nature and Conduct.* New York: Henry Holt and Co., 1922.
9. FROMM, ERICH. *Man for Himself: An Inquiry Into the Psychology of Ethics.* New York: Rinehart and Company, Inc., 1947.
10. GOLDSTEIN, KURT. *Human Nature: In the Light of Psychotherapy.* Cambridge: Harvard University Press, 1940.
11. HORNEY, KAREN. *Neurosis and Human Growth.* New York: W. W. Norton & Company, Inc., 1950.
12. KELLEY, EARL C. *Education for What Is Real.* New York: Harper & Brothers, 1947.
13. LECKY, PRESCOTT. *Self-Consistency: A Theory of Personality.* Frederick C. Thorne (ed.). New York: Island Press, 1951.
14. LOEB, LEO. *The Biological Basis of Individuality.* Springfield, Illinois: Charles C Thomas, 1945.
15. MASLOW, A. H. The Instinctoid Nature of Basic Needs. *J. Personality,* 22:326-347 (March 1954).

16. MASLOW, A. H. *Toward a Psychology of Being.* New York: D. Van Nostrand Co., Inc., 1962.
17. MAY, ROLLO. *Man's Search for Himself.* New York: W. W. Norton & Co., 1953.
18. MOONEY, ROSS. Creation, Parents, and Children. *Prog. Educ.*, 1953, 31, 14-17.
19. NIEBUHR, REINHOLD. *The Self and The Dramas of History.* New York: Charles Scribner's Sons, 1955.
20. RANK, OTTO. *Will Therapy.* New York: Alfred A. Knopf, 1936.
21. RASEY, MARIE and MENGE, J. W. *What We Learn from Children.* New York: Harper & Brothers, 1956.
22. ROGERS, CARL R. *Client-Centered Therapy.* Boston: Houghton Mifflin Co., 1951.
23. ROGERS, CARL R. *On Becoming A Person.* Boston: Houghton Mifflin Co., 1961.

# 2

## The Sense of Self

The first requirement for the growth of the individual self is that the person remain in touch with his own perceptions. No matter how different one's experience is from that of others, he must trust in the validity of his own senses if he is to evolve as a unique being. Only the person can fully know what he sees, what he hears, and what he feels to be fundamentally true. To the extent that he respects the authenticity of his own experience, he will be open to new levels of learning, to new pathways of relatedness to others, and to a genuine respect for all life.

When the person is guided by the real nature of his own experience, he also is genuinely present in his meetings with others. He is ready, as a whole person, to enter into the world of another person and to share his own resources and talents—not as a separate being, but in full communion. Genuine relating is a process of intuitive awareness, sensing, and knowing—not an intellectual, objective, detached thought process which judges and classifies the other person. Genuine relating involves a recognition of the mystery and awe, the capriciousness and unpredictability of life. It means trusting unknown developments in experience and a willingness to follow the uncertain course that results in a creative realization of one's own potentialities.

My own approach to human relations has been a growing awareness of the significance of mystery and uncertainty in life, an awareness of the value of suffering and grief as well as joy and happiness, an awareness of the power of silence in the deep moments of experience.

Once, as I sat with a person, I concentrated on his every word and motion, deliberately trying to comprehend his exact meanings. Using my resources to understand, to see through and beyond his fumbling ways and distortions of reality into his basic intentions and feelings, I tried to help him release inner tensions, to achieve a sense of inner harmony, and to restore his integrity. I tried to understand, to clarify, to say just the right words which would bring him to a higher level of comfort or comprehension. If only I could have helped him to see how in renouncing his own wishes and interests and ways he had denied his unique heritage and destiny. If only I could have helped him realize that he was a worthy self and that even though everything else were lost, he still existed as a self and this existence could never be taken away. To realize, to understand, to see with greater clarity, deeper meaning and insight, to bring the pieces together into a comprehensible whole—on these depended my success or failure in psychotherapy.

But what was being clarified? What was being understood? And what did the uncovering of missing links and relinking the whole provide? What did examination of a relationship render? Only a self in pursuit of understanding itself? Only a series of responses and interactions and influences? Only an unbroken chain of associations and events? Only an organization of discrete items? Only a clarification of what one says and does, of habits and attitudes, of projection and defenses? Is this a life being lived fully in the human sense? Is this a self growing as a self, in touch with inner resources and in correspondence with nature and other selves?

There is no doubt that the unique human gifts of logic and reasoning are of great value in clarifying ideas, understanding basic causes and motivations, solving problems, uncovering hidden meanings, meeting challenges, and making decisions. But reasoning and logic are only pieces of man engaged in certain kinds of intercourse with the universe. There are also the experiences of pain and suffering; of love and beauty; of the sun, the stars, the mountains, and the seas. There is faith in God, and the food I share with my brother, and the walk I take on a silent moonlit night, and the games I play with my children. There is loneliness and sense of being apart—even when part of a group life. Are there not many, many human experiences beyond logic and beyond reason, in which it takes courage to live with oneself or to share with others, long before there is any understanding or insight or clarification, long before there is any separated knowledge and comprehension?

There are many situations in which I am totally involved as a person—isolated hours of quiet self-reflection, lonely self experiences, moments with a congenial friend. And there are times when I feel related to a falling leaf, to an isolated flower on a frosty day, to thunder and wind and rain, when all is related to all and belongs to all and remains as it is. William Wordsworth (7) conveys such a sense of self in this poem:

> I have felt
> A presence that disturbs me with the joy
> Of elevated thought; a sense sublime
> Of something far more deeply interfused,
> Whose dwelling is the light of setting suns,
> And the round ocean and the living air,
> And the blue sky, and in the mind of man—
> A motion and a spirit, that impels
> All thinking things, all objects of all thought,
> And rolls through all things.

Are experiences like these not important in the creation of the self? Yet where is the understanding and the comprehension? What concept or definition, what thoughtful essay could ever communicate the wonder and awe of holistic experience when man is man and a tree is a tree, and the dawn is the dawn, yet each merges into the other, and each gives meaning to the other, and in unity they create something entirely new, a poetry of living form.

A breakthrough or emergence in the creation of self is expressed in the following experience of a woman who had suffered deeply and painfully before a sudden, strange submission and awakening (1, pp. 325-329).

> . . . . The pain and tension deep in the core and centre of my being was so great that I felt as might some creature which had outgrown its shell, and yet could not escape. What it was I knew not, that it was a great yearning—for freedom, for larger life—for deeper love. There seemed to be no response in nature to that infinite need. The great tide swept on uncaring, pitiless, and strength gone, every resource exhausted, nothing remained but *submission*. . . .

At last, subdued, with a curious, growing strength in my weakness, I *let go of myself!* In a short time, to my surprise, I began to feel a sense of physical comfort, of rest, as if some strain or tension was removed. Never before had I experienced such a feeling of perfect health. . . .

How long that period of intense rapture lasted I do not know—it seemed an eternity—it might have been but a few moments. Then came relaxation, the happy tears, the murmured, rapturous expression. . . .

I had learned the grand lesson, that suffering is the price which must be paid for all that is worth having; that in some mysterious way we are refined and sensitized, doubtless largely by it, so that we are made susceptible to nature's higher and finer influences—this, if true of one, is true of all. And feeling and knowing this, I do not now rave as once I did, but am "silent" as I sit and look out upon all the sorrow of the world. . . .

There was and is still, though not so noticeable as earlier, a very decided and peculiar feeling across the brow above the eyes, as of tension gone, a feeling of *more room.* That is the physical sensation. The mental is a sense of majesty, of serenity, which is more noticeable *when out of doors.* Another very decided and peculiar effect followed the phenomena above described—that of being centred, or of being a centre. . . . I was anchored at last! But to what? To something outside myself? . . . .

My feeling is as if I were as distinct and separate from all other beings and things as is the moon in space and at the same time indissolubly one with all nature.

Out of this experience was born an unfaltering trust. Deep in the soul, below pain, below all the distraction of life, is a silence vast and grand—an infinite ocean of calm, which nothing can disturb; nature's own exceeding peace, which "passes understanding."

That which we seek with passionate longing, here and there, upward and outward, we find at last *within ourselves.* The kingdom within! The indwelling God! are words whose sublime meaning we never shall fathom.

Many, many self experiences are a mystery. One can participate in them, share them, live them in the existential sense. But it is absurd to try to understand what is inexplicable; to derive meaning, motivation, purpose, and goal from what is simple and clear. What is a mystery is a mystery—life is a mystery, and death, and creation of the self and of the universe. It is this mystery, this unknown ecstasy of life that in present-day changing society is not wholeheartedly embraced and valued, but too often ignored, neglected—or merely analyzed and understood. Albert Guérard (3, pp. 154-155) speaks of this universal mysticism in his book, *Bottle in the Sea:*

> . . . . whether you think in terms of a grace parsimoniously imparted from above, or of a seed growing through the whole of mankind, the mystic experience, in its full directness and intensity, is rare in our days, and it is uncertain. Not only are ordinary mortals skeptical about such a transcendental gift, but the favored ones themselves have their hours of doubt and despair. . . .
>
> Like Descartes's *good sense,* like the aesthetic response, *mysticism is universal.* Every man, at some moment of his existence, be it ever so humble, or, far worse, be it ever so hectic, has felt its irresistible power. But we feel it in utter darkness. The ineffable imposes silence. It cannot be comprehended, it cannot be remembered, it leaves no intelligible trace. There remains with us only an undefinable longing for a truth, for a peace, for a love passing all understanding. Metaphysics, theology, by rational means; ritual, by material ones, are attempts to end the quest. What they offer is but a painted screen, a *trompe-l'oeil* claiming to be the ultimate reality. . . . There is more faith diffused through the whole of mankind than in the rare and magnificent flashes of the professed mystics. Seers, poets, and conquerors are portents: we are awed by their unique power. But spiritual life is not made up of portents: it is an obscure and constant endeavor.

It is this dimension—call it spiritual or mystic or aesthetic, or creative, or simply man being man. I am speaking about unknown forces in man merging with unknown forces in the universe and letting happen what will, permitting reality to emerge in its fullest sense and letting the unpredictable in oneself encounter the unpredictable in the other. Then a breakthrough of self occurs in which man does the unexpected and emerges newly born, perceiving, sensing and experiencing in a totally different way.

How can the individual develop latent resources and hidden talents when he is urged to conform, to compete, to achieve, to evaluate, to establish fixed goals? How can the uniqueness of the person take form in a living situation, when he is pressured to communicate in precise ways and to model himself along the usual norms and standards, to complete certain developmental tasks?

We live in an age of reasoning in which the self is a self system, a series of rationalities and concepts, in which skills are used to exploit and manipulate, in which abstractions are more relevant than the realities abstracted and in which the symbol has become more real than the person or thing symbolized. Ours is an age of comfort, ready to receive and consume, in which it is easier to stay within the known and safe limits of life than it is to plunge into new relations and experiences; in which it is safer to accept the usual and regular facts in the usual and regular ways; in which it is better to keep quiet and look away whenever there is a vibrant cry for justice and truth; in which it is better to remain on the edges of a real relationship because a genuine meeting might bring pain, suffering, and grief as well as joy and happiness. We live at a time when a calm, deliberate, reasonable voice is heeded while spontaneous excitement, joy, enthusiasm, emotional fervor and cries for justice are all interpreted as signs of immaturity, hostility, selfishness, or projections of sexual deprivation. We live in a time of machines and technological advances and techniques and procedures, when one can get a list of approved ways to speak and act for almost any situation. We live in an age of adjustment when the individual is forced into group modes and preferences—either by authority or popular vote.

Unanimity, however, is neither practical nor expedient, because individual differences not only create a split within the individual but a breach between himself and others as well. Neither the group nor the individual can grow and develop fully without the other. There is no way to realize the full possibilities in group life as long as one person is rejected, minimized, ignored or treated as an inferior or outcast. To the extent that there is malice toward one person, ill-will and ill-feeling spread. Every person in the group is inflicted and is powerless to channel available resources into creative expression. One cannot carry evil thoughts, feelings, and intentions in his heart without at the same time deterring and restraining himself in his own purposes or directions. One, therefore, must live through and work out one's state of rejecting or being rejected before group life can contain a depth of spirit, devotion, and authentic communality. The personal issues and disputes in the challenge of the individual confronting the group must first be met. Otherwise, the split in the group prevents each man from deriving a sense of integrity and of wholeness. Only by learning to live with the deviant one, by recognizing his right to be, and respecting the issues he raises or the problems he creates, can a high level of group living be realized. The personal matters must be settled first. Social or group life then follows.

We are dissatisfied with the meaningless motions, habits, and goals of modern life and the estrangement that results from impersonal study and attempts to understand rather than living imminently in the requirements or challenges of each situation.

We live in an age of analysis, yet it is never the "why" that really matters. The "why" can only help one prepare for or soften a situation. The "why" is a kind of rational sop. It is not part of the battle for truth. It is not the living experience but only an indirect substitute.

The man who accepts life as a whole does not need to measure or understand or know why. This is the theme of the following poem from Witter Bynner's *The Way of Life According to Laotzu* (2, p. 21).

> The surest test if a man be sane
> Is if he accepts life whole, as it is,
> Without needing by measure or touch to understand
> The measureless untouchable source
> Of its images,
> The measureless untouchable source
> Of its substances,
> The source which, while it appears dark emptiness,
> Brims with a quick force
> Farthest away
> And yet nearest at hand
> From oldest time unto this day,
> Charging its images with origin:
> What more need I know of the origin
> Than this?

The supreme fact of existence is the reality itself, the experience—*this* illness, *this* conflict, *this* ecstasy, *this* life, *this* death, *this* moment transcending other moments. It is *this* realm of human experience, of immediate personal existence, whether in love or solitude, whether in suffering or despair in which the self grows. But man cannot be aware of the meaning of experience while experiencing in an integrated way. Understanding of experience comes later, but it is incidental to experience itself. Kenneth Patton (5, pp. 18-19) comes to a similar conviction, as expressed in the following excerpt:

> Words, our own or another's, can never be more than a commentary upon living experience. Reading can never be substituted for living. What do I understand about a tree? I have climbed into the branches and felt the trunk sway in the winds, and I have hidden among the leaves like an apple. I have lain among the branches and ridden them like another bough, and I have torn the skin of my hands and the cloth of my trousers climbing up and down the harsh bark. I have peeled away the skin of the willow and fondled the white, sweet wood, and my ax has bitten through the pure fibers, and my saw laid bare the yearly rings and the heart-wood. Through the microscope I have copied out the traceries of the cells, and I have shaken out the rootlets like hair upon my hand; and I have chewed the gum and curled my tongue around the syrup, and shredded the wood fibers with my teeth. I have lain among the autumn leaves and my nostrils drank the smoke of their sacrifice. I have planed the yellow lumber and driven in the nails, and polished the smooth driftwood with my palm.
>
> Within me now there is a grainyness, a leafiness, a confluence of roots and branches, forests above and afar off, and a light soil made of a thousand years of their decay, and this whisper, this memory of fingers and nostrils, the fragile leaf-budding shivering within my eyes. What is my understanding of trees if it is not this reality lying behind these poor names? So do the lips, the tongue, the eyes and ears and fingers gather their voices and speak inwardly to the understanding. If I am wise I do not try to take another into that strange, placeless place of my thoughts, but I lead him to the forest and lose him among the trees, until he finds the trees within himself, and finds himself within the trees.

Many efforts to direct, predict, or control are in reality flights from experience or forms of self-denial. In actuality man is not predictable; man is forever impermanent.

Though he exists in a substantial way, he is always discovering new avenues of expression—not only because there are many ways in which he can develop his potentialities but also because there are unpredictable forces in the universe and in other men that influence his development and his experience. No matter how genuine a relationship may be, there will always be stresses and storms, to bring unexpected words, to make one impotent and afraid, to make one feel the terribleness of not being able to count on the other person, to create the despairing feeling that breaks in love can never be repaired. But one lives and loves, and suffers and forgets, and begins again—perhaps even thinking that this time, this new time, is to be permanent. But man is not permanent and man is not predictable.

It is the mystery of the reality that matters. Not why it exists, but that it exists. Not why I suffer, but that I suffer. Not why I feel empty and cold and lonely, but that I am lonely and cold and afraid. Not why I am joyous and loving, but that I feel joy and love. Not why my spirit runs with the wind, but that I have suddenly awakened to an alive beauty that I have never experienced before. Not why I must die, but dying itself. The existential moments of life do not contain a why, but only the reality that man is constructed as he is.

Experiences of mystery and impermanence and the unexpected do not occur because man wishes or wills them. In the beginning man is born with certain potentialities, predispositions, and tendencies; and in fulfilling these he makes choices. His reality is not a reality that he chooses, but a reality that is ultimately a mystery, created by the unknown. At times, man can choose to be or not be, to grow as a self or to develop a pseudo-self that adopts the expectations and ways of others, wearing masks and incorporating ghosts. But the question of free choice and self determination becomes relevant only if the growing self is severely denied or threatened with disapproval or rejection; or if it is confronted with an issue, challenge, question, or problem. Not all human situations, however, are confrontations and not every act of the self grows out of challenge. In most cases, development of the self is spontaneous with the individual naturally using whatever resources are available in his immediate, personal experience.

The way in which I am constructed, the fact that I am a particular individual, limits me but at the same time enables me to experience in unique ways. The evolution of the self is an act of self-creation not the accumulating of insight and understanding. This fundamental truth of the self can be realized only if the individual is willing and courageous enough to follow to some natural conclusion this moment of experience, this conviction, this ideal, this living encounter, this facing the unknown and participating with the total commitment of the self. Such expression, such passion for life may emerge in written, spoken, graphic, or aesthetic forms; in relation or in isolation; in I-Thou encounters; and in silent, inner experience. Not a priori theories, principles, or techniques, but rather a compassionate willingness is required—as is the courage to live before the fact, before the understanding, before any rational support or certainty, to live the moment to its natural peak and conclusion, and to accept with dignity whatever joy, grief, misfortune, or unexpectedness occurs.

A friend of mine, who worked in a residential hospital with emotionally disturbed children, met the children in just this open existential sense. I should like to share with you one of her experiences, which she relates in her own words:

> One day Mark came into the playroom, looked at me and said, "There is a very ugly song going through my head, through my head, all the time." When asked to tell more about it, he said it was about the Muscle Man and he sang several bars. He continued, "It really is such a bad song, and it gives me so much trouble. Would you take me for a walk up our back road and sing to me about The Silvery Moon, to see if I can get rid of such a bad song?" With hand pressed tight in mine we walked among the beautiful autumn coloring. Everywhere the reds and yellows and golden browns surrounded us and at each step I was urged to sing: "Please sing again The Silvery Moon." Soon I was joined by a small voice and we continued our walk. After some minutes I felt the small hand slip from mine, and the feet that were heavily

trudging became light, and Mark ran ahead and called back to me,

"The day is bea-u-ti-ful,
It is blue up there
And blue down here
I am up there
I am everywhere
Where it is blue.
The day is beau-ti-ful!"

Mark slipped back to my side and continued,

"The sky is blue and not black
The wind is soft and not hard
The clouds are white and not black
*Sech* a bea-u-ti-ful day
No more doggone ugly songs
Going round and round in my head."

Soon we came to the brook that always holds special delight for Mark. We sat together quietly listening to the flowing waters and Mark looked at me saying, "Now I feel this much happy [holding his hands far apart]. I am happy because you are happy and because I am with you."

It was time to return and as we both reluctantly left the soothing waters Mark said, "Sing our song once more please, because it makes me happy instead of sad; it makes me good instead of bad; it makes me warm instead of cold; it makes me skip instead of walk. It is a bea-u-ti-ful day to be out!"

This is an experience of self-creation, an experience of utter mystery, between two selves, each responsible for his own destiny and yet related in a genuine way.

Ultimately, I cannot be responsible for another person. I can only participate in his life, no matter what that participation may come to mean to him. But, in the end he discovers his own meanings, his own resources, his own nature, his own being. Laurens van der Post (6, pp. 164-165) catches this feeling exactly in the following passages from *Venture to the Interior:*

It had been perfect for them on the mountain. There, and in themselves, they found everything they had ever wanted; and in this perfection they meant to live till the end. She almost gave me the impression that they were refugees from their own past, thinking they could rid themselves of the problem of their lives by changing their location; believing they only had to go far enough away and they would leave their problem behind them. How little those unfortunate children knew of the hound of unfulfilled nature within the blood that is forever on our trail, ready to aid and abet the dark fates without.

Now I shall never know any more detail about the life of that brave, upright young man; but it seems to me certain from what I know already, that sooner or later there was bound to be a reckoning between himself and his nature which I could not influence, save as an instrument of the inevitable. On Friday at ten-thirty in the Great Ruo gorge of Mlanje the unpredictable in himself and the unpredictable in the mountain, the split in himself and the dark gash in Mlanje met and became one. . . . That moment in the gorge has become a part of me. I shall have to live with it to the end of my life. Nor is it the only moment of its kind. There have been quite a number of other moments equally grim. Of these I need say no more now, except perhaps that they have a habit of all massing together and presenting themselves to my senses at the most unexpected moments; waking me up at midnight, making me hesitate in my steps across a crowded street, or perhaps just making me stroke the head of a neighbour's dog with unusual tenderness.

When they do that it is necessary to relive them again in some way, to look them squarely in their eyes, to take them by the hand in an avowal of a sad friendship, and say "How are you now? Better? Is there anything more I can do for you?" and at a shake of a dark head, to reply encouragingly before continuing on one's way, "Perhaps it will be better next time. Perhaps it will pass." This does not sound much. But it is all one can do, and it helps even if it does not cure.

Now when I meet with a person I am no longer concerned with helping or curing him—not as a professional worker with theories and systems and rubrics and techniques. I am not even concerned with trying to understand him, but only in being with him—as a human being who is willing to let imagination and comprehension, mental capabilities, and compassion mingle freely, and to let the destiny of two lives proceed within the mystery and unpredictable nature of two growing selves engaged in immediate personal experience.

## REFERENCES

1. BUCKE, RICHARD M. *Cosmic Consciousness.* New York: E. P. Dutton and Co., Inc., 1901.
2. BYNNER, WITTER. *The Way of Life According to Laotzu.* New York: John Day Co., 1944.
3. GUÉRARD, ALBERT. *Bottle in the Sea.* Cambridge, Massachusetts: Harvard University Press, 1954.
4. MOUSTAKAS, CLARK. Creativity, Conformity, and The Self in *Creativity and Psychological Health,* ed. by Michael Andrews. New York: Syracuse University Press, 1961.
5. PATTON, KENNETH L. *Man's Hidden Search.* Boston: Meeting House Press, 1954.
6. VAN DER POST, LAURENS. *Venture to the Interior.* New York: Penguin Books, 1957.
7. WORDSWORTH, WILLIAM. *Poetical Works.* Boston: Hurd and Houghton, 1877, Vol. II.

# 3

# Creativity and Conformity

Many times in my life I have been faced with a dilemma that, after much internal struggle and deliberation, turned out to be illusory. I continually discovered that only one pathway was open, that there was only one way to go—a way that grew out of my own self. The problem turned out to be not one of resolving a situation that called for a choice between unsatisfactory alternatives, but rather a question of bringing into being what already existed as self-potential, that is, it required bringing into being my own identity as it related to the challenge of a crucial situation. It is this experience of expressing and actualizing one's individual identity in an integrated form in communion with one's self, with nature, and with other persons that I call creative.

Every facet of the universe, each man, woman, child, each plant and animal, the clouds and heavenly bodies, the wind and the sand and stars, each object, each space, even bits of gravel and broken stone, each item of nature, contains its own particular identity, its own unique form, its own special existence. Every aspect of nature and life contains its own spark of originality that attains a living unity and persistence of form through its relation to other identities and forms.

In the beginning there is the individual with his own matchless identity. He emerges. He takes his stand. He brings his identity into being through authentic encounters, through genuine meetings. He grows and discovers himself in experiences with other persons, with physical matters, with living forms. His identity comes into relief as he breathes his own spirit into everything he touches, as he relates significantly and openly with others and with the universe. This is the message in Kahlil Gibran's aphorism (8, p. 17): "Should you really open your eyes and see, you would behold your image in all images. And should you open your ears and listen, you would hear your own voice in all voices."

Growth of individual identity in open relatedness; creation of being in vital experiences with other beings; ingestion of meaning, feeling, belief, value, within a unique self—this is the challenging responsibility and essential creativity in all of life. Martin Buber (1, pp. 139-140) expresses the indelible creativity of man as follows:

> Every person born into this world represents something new, something that never existed before, something original and unique. It is the duty of every person . . . to know . . . that there has never been anyone like him in the world, for if there had been someone like him, there would have been no need for him to be in the world. Every single man is a new thing in the world and is called upon to fulfill his particularity in this world.

Each real self maintains a certain substance, consistency, and autonomy of self while at the same time evolving self-insights, meanings, and integrations. Whatever a man says or does, however alienated, detached, and unrelated he may become, there remains within him forever an entirely unique and particular substance that is his own, which is intact and inviolate. This substance can be recognized and called forth in an encounter with other persons or forms in the universe.

To be creative means to experience life in one's own way, to perceive from one's own person, to draw upon one's own resources, capacities, roots. It means facing life directly and honestly; courageously searching for and discovering grief, joy, suffering, pain, struggle, conflict, and finally inner solitude.

Only from the search into oneself can the creative emerge. The creator must often be a world unto himself, finding everything within himself and in his relations with others to whom he is attached (21). This is the theme in Laotzu's (2, p. 55) poem:

> There is no need to run outside
> For better seeing,
> Nor to peer from a window. Rather abide
> At the center of your being;
> For the more you leave it, the less you learn.
> Search your heart and see

If he is wise who takes each turn:
The way to do is to be.

According to Theodore Reik, Freud's essential creativity was his talent for searching within. Reik (20, pp. 263-264) says:

> . . . what will forever separate Freud's way from that of other psychoanalysts . . . is that his discoveries were made by himself. They were the triumph of a mind in search of itself, which, in reaching its aims, discovered the laws governing the emotional processes of all minds. We learn these discoveries with the help of books and lectures; we make them again, rediscover them, when we are in the process of analysis—that is, when we are analyzed or when we analyze others. Our psychoanalytic institutes seem to be unaware of the fact that being analyzed cannot compete in experience value with unearthing these insights oneself. The one experience cannot be likened to the other . . . One's own psychoanalysis—however important, indeed indispensable, for the understanding of oneself and others—is, of course, not comparable to the process by which Freud arrived at his results by a heroic mental deed, by a victory over his own inner reluctances and resistances. When we are analyzed by others, it is an entirely different process, induced from outside even when we ask for it ourselves. It lacks the intimacy and the depth of experience felt in discovering one's secrets oneself. Nothing said to us, nothing we can learn from others, reaches us so deep as that which we find in ourselves.

In the creative experience, every moment is unique, and contains the potentiality for original expression. There are two basic requirements: that the person be direct, honest, consistent in his own feelings and his own convictions; and that he feel a genuine devotion to life, a feeling of belonging and knowing. Creativity is an abstraction that attains a meaningful, concrete form in a particular and unique relation. The branches of a tree stretch out expansive and free, maintaining a basic identity, an essential uniqueness in color, form, and pattern. They stand out in contrast to the fixed nature of the trunk. Yet one cannot see a tree without recognizing its essential harmony, its wholeness, and its unity. Each facet attains its identity and remains a living creation within a genuine whole, within an organic communion.

An experience of unusual communion is recorded by Kelman in his essay, *Communing and Relating* (10, pp. 74-75):

> I was sitting in an isolated spot on a log late one afternoon watching the brilliance of the setting sun behind the volcanoes. At that hour the lake surface was like glass and no one was on it. Not a leaf stirred. The only occasional sound, as external evidence of movement, was of a bird in flight. I do not know how long I had been sitting there when to my left, about fifty yards away, down a path, soundlessly, in their bare feet and in their native costume, came a father and his three-year-old son. They were holding hands. At the lake shore the father lifted the little boy into a boat and then got in beside him. They sat there motionless until it was almost dark. The father lifted the little boy out, took his hand, and walked up the path until they were lost to my view.
>
> Throughout I heard not a sound, saw no expressions on the face of either indicating that they were talking to one another or had even turned to look at one another. How long they or I sat there, or how much time elapsed between my arrival and my return up the path to the village, I cannot say. By the clock it might have been several hours. Feelingwise it was a moment and eternity. The feeling of stillness and being still outside of myself and to a degree inside of myself was palpable, tangible, concrete. While it was going on there were feelings of awesomeness and wonder as well as of unease. Watching and being a part of this whole event, I felt as though I were intruding on a sacred rite. Maybe it was part of their religious practices, for rituals around the rising and the setting of the sun are common. And, in fact, at the base of the highest volcano is a small hill in which many archaeological treasures have been found. From ancient times the Indians have called it *Cerro de Oro*, hill of gold. Maybe I was part of a sacred rite, of a father being with a son in the ultimate of intimacy, which is communing.

Not all relatedness emerges from a sense of harmony and communion. It sometimes begins with an issue, or conflict, or sense of deviation, or separateness. This was my experience last winter on a cold blustering day. It was a severe winter which exceeded records for frigid temperatures, ice formations, and accumulations of snow. The cold, noisy, violence of a raging wind kept me indoors. After almost two days of internment, I began to feel dull and almost completely insensible to the children's play and other events going on around me. Everything seemed colorless and toneless.

I felt trapped by the violent storm outside. The wind came swaggering through the walls and lashed against the windows, reverberating the panes, and echoing throughout the house. Screaming, fluttering sounds came through the weather stripping of the doors. Yet these auditory vibrations barely entered my center of awareness. I had been taught that the safest place in a blizzard was the warm comfort of home. And this had been my retreat for almost two days, not out of choice, but from tradition and fear. I was annoyed that a wild and fitful wind had forced me into an asylum and that I had conformed in the ordinary and intelligent way.

But something was wrong. The household scenes were gloomy. I saw only the coverings and felt the lethargy and boredom of a static life. The more I thought about my situation, the more restless I became. A growing inner feeling surged within me and I decided to face the wind. I had never been in a blizzard before by choice, but in that moment I decided to enter the turbulent outside. Immediately I experienced an exhilarating and exciting feeling. I stood before the bitter, cold, turbulent flow of wind, a wind that was inciting retreat and withdrawal in every direction. Momentarily I was stung and pushed back. I hesitated, uncertain whether I could move forward. It was a tremendous challenge. Holding my ground, I stood in the way of the wind. We met head-on. I knew for the first time the full meaning of a severe wind. I felt it in every pore of my body but realized I would not retreat. I stood firm and gradually, slowly I began to move forward in spite of the violent, shattering gusts which emerged repeatedly to block my path. Tears fell down my face. It was a painful experience but at the same time wonderfully refreshing and joyous. It was cold, yet I was warmed by a tremendous surge of emotion. I felt radiant and alive as I continued my journey. As the wind met me and moved me, I became aware of the whole atmosphere—like a powerful dynamo; crackling, crunching, clanging noises everywhere; a rushing, swaying, churning turbulence; a world charged with electric fury. For the first time in my life I truly understood the meaning of a blizzard.

All about me were shining elements and sharp, penetrating sounds which I could see, and hear, and feel without effort. It was an awesome feeling, witnessing the wild turbulence. Everything was charged with life and beauty. The meeting with the wind revived me and restored me to my own resourcefulness. I felt an expansive and limitless energy.

I returned home. Everything took on a shining light and a spark of beauty. I played ecstatically with my children, with a burst of enthusiasm and excitement. I seemed to be inexhaustible. I made repairs, painted, helped with the evening meal, assisted with the children's baths and bedtime, and spent a joyous evening reading and conversing with my wife. Out of the tumultuous experience, I found new joy in life, new energy, uniqueness and beauty. I had conquered my lethargy and discovered a lively affinity in everything I touched. Everything which had been dull and commonplace took on a living splendor. I realized how out of the wild, confused, turbulent experience, came a sense of inner exaltation, peace, symmetry, and a recognition of the vital manifestations of life; how out of the initial conflict came a sense of individual aliveness and a feeling of harmony and relatedness to a raging wind.

Using a different form, in the following poems, fourth grade children express their sense of harmony and relatedness to nature:

I thought I saw Spring,
Outside peeping around a cloud,
It was pretty, very pretty,
With buds on the trees
And flowers peeping out on the ground,
With the snow almost gone
And grass looking on,
I knew, I knew I saw Spring (22).

The trees look like little cradles rocking
With little babies inside,
And the soft wind blowing
The soft, soft music playing sweetly (6).

I felt the wind hitting my face
I felt the leaves
And with the wind the cold and ice
Wonderful world we live in, that has so many ways (7).

When I looked out the window this morning I saw trees and houses
The trees were bare and wind blew and blew
Then it was calm and then I felt happy.
Spring was coming, I knew it.
The houses were quiet,
I saw an old bird's nest, it wasn't making a home for a family of birds. It was just there.
No smoke came out of the chimney
Spring was coming. Spring was here (24).

In the month of March, I feel like a tree with no leaves
I feel cold like the wind, the breeze of a fan, the dirt under the snow.
I feel like the wind helping the kites along
Making the trees grow
Blowing free (18).

Creativity is not adaptation. It always involves a solemn compact between one's self and others or between one's self and the raw materials of nature and life. It is a pure form of self-other relatedness. However different, strange, and unordinary one's way may appear to others, when it is a genuine self-living and growing, it is also authentically related.

The creative moment is unique. It has never occurred before and can never exist again. Every genuine moment is its own creative fulfillment and maintains a timeless existence.

What I am pointing to is something altogether unconditioned and transcendent of all effort, motive, or determination. It is an ultimate, universal, concrete reality that is individual yet related, harmonious yet discordant, congruent yet dissimilar. The creative cannot be scaled down to the level of facts or observable data. It rides on the horizons and fills the heavens. It is incomparable and can never be subsumed under categories of definition, communication, and logic.

I have selected a number of examples to illustrate the meaning of creativity and the creative experience. The first of these was written by Janet Petersen (18), a classroom teacher.

At morning-time,
A quiet, hushed anticipation;
And all around, a thrilling tingling expectation
Of a new day!
The slow, yet steady hum of voices;
Humor here,
Sadness there,
Serious, deliberate conversation;
Not one voice without its special meaning;
Not one meeting without its permanent engraving on the
whole of my being!
Then the quiet, hushed relaxation,
The silent-time for reflection;
The night-time;
The dark-room of my life,
Where the new being develops,
That eagerly, anxiously awaits
A new day!

A seventh grade student, Janie Cassady (4) wrote:

The first creation was when "In the beginning God created Heaven and Earth." But since then man has been creating every day. Everyone creates something. Even if you were locked in a padded room with just pills to eat you would create something if only a dream of getting out and eating solid food.

Michael Angelo, Leonardo da Vinci, Rubins created beautiful masterpieces which will live through the ages. Carl Sandburg, Walt Whitman, Edgar Allan Poe, James Whitcomb Riley created poems which will last forever. But ordinary people like you and I are the greatest creators of all. We create something far more important than paintings and poems. We create love. Everyone loves something and everyone creates love.

Yes, in the beginning "God created Heaven and Earth" but after that "God created Man" thus creating *LOVE*.

Another seventh grade student, Don Camph (3) conveyed his understanding of creativity as follows:

Creativity is the ability to create experience—to make joy and sorrow, to rejoice and to mourn. It is not just building skyscrapers, and having a brilliant intellect, and creating masterpieces but it is being able to set men's hearts afire when they are in despair, being able to cheer them when they are sad, and most of all being able to create friends.

From the same grade, Ron Miller (14) wrote:

> Some things may not be beautiful or great,
> But if it is your own work,
> Your original self,
> It is creative.

David, a 9-year-old, whose intelligence was questioned by the school because of poor achievement, perceived in a creative way. In his fourth and fifth therapy sessions, pointing out the window of my office, the following conversation occurred (16):

D: Look, everything so fresh and green. That's a special feeling. It sort of brings me close to everything, you know, feels sort of spiritual, everything I see. Everything seems like it's available and the way things are. It seems natural, like I've seen it all my life.

MR. M: Something very close and yet familiar, unlike what most people see.

D: See that road out there? You might think it was something different if people didn't call it a road and say what it was for. You might see it as a pattern or a contrast to something else out there. You could put it in your own thinking and imagining. You could make a design that fits with everything else.

MR. M: Yes, everything comes together.

D: And you just see designs. If you really look you can see a design in everything—like that curving branch and the ones below it form a pattern. If you don't separate them, they fade together in a dimension. You see designs in the formation of everything out there.

MR. M: It's different from—

D: What others say are real things. It kind of takes it away when you're told it's not that way. When I was littler, I didn't have a learned sense of perspective and I saw things differently.

MR. M: Now you have to concentrate to see the shape and form of things as they really are.

D: Yeah, there's a particular feeling that comes along with those designs. Everything comes together. It seems like everything is available. I just look at all of it like it was together and I'm kind of glad I'm in the world, you know.

Mr. M: It's a beautiful feeling when we don't have to see life separate and apart, just to be free to experience life in all its availability.

D: I wish I had words like the Wintu Indians do. They have words for feelings. It's like saying, "Going downstairs." They would say, "Going downstairs him" you know. Sort of brings past and future together in the present, like "going downstairness," or "going downstairsness him." It brings all of time together.

Mr. M: Sort of unity of time in one experience.

D: And with the spiritual. It's not motion like our words say, like going and coming and moving.

Mr. M: But a feeling, an experience. When everything is coming alive, growing, open.

D: Yeah. It's very—very—it brings you close to spiritual things. You're not in touch with any matter except the matter you see. Sort of brings me in touch with everything.

I believe it is the real feelings, within a vital experience, in an intimate relation to nature or other selves, that constitute the creative encounter. When a person's involvement in a situation is based on appearances, expectations, or the standards of others; when he acts in a conventional manner, or according to prescribed roles and functions, when he is concerned with status and approval; his growth as a creative self is impaired. When the individual is conforming, following, imitating, being like others, he moves increasingly in the direction of self-alienation. Such a person fears issues and controversies. He fears standing out or being different. He does not think through his experience to find value or meaning, does not permit himself to follow his own perceptions to some natural conclusion. He avoids directly facing disputes and becomes anxious in situations which require self-awareness and self-discovery. He becomes increasingly similar until his every act erases his real identity and beclouds his uniqueness. Maslow (12) points out that the only way such a person can achieve safety, order, lack of threat, lack of anxiety, is through orderliness, predictability, control, and mastery. If the conformist can proceed into the future on the basis of "well-tried" rules, habits, and modes of adjustment which have worked in the past (and which he insists on using in the future), he feels safe. But he experiences deep anxiety when he faces a new situation, when he cannot predetermine his behavior, when he does not know the acceptable form.

Gradually the conforming person loses touch with himself, with his own real feelings. He becomes unable to experience in a genuine way, and suffers inwardly from a dread of nothingness until finally despair nails him to himself. The torment will remain because he cannot get rid of himself. To be a self is the greatest concession made to man, but at the same time it is eternity's demand upon him (11).

In conformity, life has no meaning for there is no true basis for existence. Cut off from his own real wishes and capacities, the individual experiences no fulfillment and no sense of authentic relatedness. He strives to achieve safety and status. He strives to overcome his natural desires and to gain a victory over his natural surroundings. His goals are acquisition and control. Separated from nature and others yet appearing to be in harmony with them, he takes his cues from the designated authority figures. A young woman in psychotherapy has recognized this pattern (25).

> So you have to put everything out . . . as a question, you know. Because he's the one who knows and we're the ones who don't know. You can't (pause) you're sort of stepping onto his territory if you start giving out with pronouncements of facts. You see, what you're doing is you're competing, you're being disrespectful. You're moving into his position which—you just *don't do* that. . . . And I know that very well, but how I know it or why I know it —you see, I don't know it as intellectual concept—I just *know* it. My father didn't allow anybody but himself to be the lawgiver and statement maker. . . . And a lot of those things I know, I don't know in words, I just know.

The conformist has been forced into denying the self, not as the result of existential or valid social limits, but rather as a result of the frequent experiences of being confined, restricted, and limited. A distinction must be made here between natural limits and imposed limitations. *Limits* provide the structure through which individual identity emerges and grows. They enable the organism to use its capacities within its own defined structure and are meaningful as the inherent requirements of a situation. *Limitations* are induced and imposed from without and are external and extraneous. They are blocks and deterrents to growth and hinder creative emergence.

The conforming person does not use his own resources, his own experiences, but takes his direction from experts, authority figures, and traditional guides. Somewhere along the way he has given up his actual identity and submerged himself into acceptable group modes. He has been rejected by others as a unique, independent self and he has come to reject himself. He is cut off from vital self-resources which would enable him to grow in accordance with his talents and to find his place in the world. He has lost touch with himself.

This was the tragedy of an adult in psychotherapy, expressed beautifully in the following passages (9):

> From ten thousand miles away I saw it as a blinding light: the importance, the necessity of a Self! One's own single self. My original life—*what had happened to it?* Chaos was here—all around and in me—that I understood in all my fragments. But was that all one could ever know? What about the perfect planets, this earth, people, objects? Didn't they exist and move? Couldn't they be known? Yes . . . but there has to be a knower, a *subject*, as well! (Meaning is a bridge between *two* things.) Beginnings, direction, movement had to be *from* a single point; and ours is where we stand, alone, our being *sui generis*.
>
> Suddenly vistas spread out and out to the sky, and all came together at my feet. Was it possible that I had touched the key to the universe—the key which every man carries so nonchalantly in his pocket? Instantly I knew in my bones, and by grief itself, that I had discovered the very core and essence of neurosis—my neurosis and perhaps every neurosis. The secret of wretchedness WAS SELFLESSNESS! Deep and hidden, the fact and the fear of not having a self. Not being a self. Not-being. And at the end—actual chaos.
>
> How is it possible to lose a self? The treachery, unknown and unthinkable, begins with our secret psychic death in

childhood—if and when we are not loved and are cut off from our spontaneous wishes. (Think: What is left?) But wait—it is not just this simple murder of psyche. That might be written off, the tiny victim might even "outgrow" it—but it is a perfect double crime in which he himself also gradually and unwittingly takes part. He has not been accepted for himself, *as he is*.

Oh, they "love" him, but they want him or force him or expect him to be different! Therefore he must be *unacceptable*. He himself learns to believe it and at last even takes it for granted. He has truly given himself up. No matter now whether he obeys them, whether he clings, rebels or withdraws—his behavior, his performance is all that matters. His center of gravity is in "them", not in himself—yet if he so much as noticed that he'd think it natural enough. And the whole thing is entirely plausible; all invisible, automatic, and anonymous!

This is the perfect paradox. Everything looks normal; no crime was intended; there is no corpse, no guilt. All we can see is the sun rising and setting as usual. But what has happened? He has been rejected, not only by them, but by himself. (He is actually without a self.) What has he lost? Just the one true and vital part of himself: His own yes-feeling, which is his very capacity for growth, his root system. But alas, he is not dead. "Life" goes on, and so must he. From the moment he gives himself up, and to the extent that he does so, all unknowingly he sets about to create and maintain a pseudo-self. But this is an expediency—a "self" without wishes. This one shall be loved (or feared) where he is despised, strong where he is weak; it shall go through the motions (Oh, but they are caricatures!) not for fun or joy but for survival; not simply because it wants to move but because it has to obey. This necessity is not life—not his life—it is a defense mechanism against death. It is also the machine of death. From now on he will be torn apart by compulsive (unconscious) *needs* or ground by (unconscious) conflicts into paralysis, every motion and every instant cancelling out his being, his integrity; and all the while he is disguised as a normal person and expected to behave like one!

The individual is taught to perceive in a certain way, not his way but the way adults view things; the adult with authority, of course, perceives correctly. This begins at an early age and gradually, through repetitive conditioning and reward or fear of punishment and rejection, the individual begins to act in standard ways without being aware of conforming.

I now quote from two seventh grade children who wrote their views on conformity.

> Today there is too much effort on children conforming and being more like other people. But these people children are supposed to be like, now get this, they spend more money every year on cosmetics and alcohol than on education. And in this past year they consumed between 10 and 16 million tranquilizers. Do I want to follow slogans like, "Be like others" and "Join the group." Again, I say, "No!" I want to be an individual and think and act for myself. Why, even in a gang, we can be individuals and still be good members. We don't have to just go along with everybody else's ideas.
>
> We, the nonconformists, are sometimes thought of as abnormal by some people, but just think of that slow learning boy who was nicknamed "old father hare" and was called unsociable. Who was this? Only Albert Einstein. This was a boy who thought for himself. Our first duty to society is to be somebody, that is to say, to be ourselves.
>
> As a teacher or adult, you must think over the following questions, "When you see that the child has a difference do you think of it for his growth, or do you look at it to see how his neighbors might react?" "Do you want him to be successful or to follow his own talents even if he is lonely and poverty stricken? Is your child doing things against his own judgment, just because others do it or is he free to follow his own mind and ideas? You can tell if you are forcing a child to conform.
>
> There are many times when I was made to conform when I needed to be encouraged to be myself. Last year my teacher made me conform to her many times. I was bored in class because you couldn't do anything as an individual. My parents made me conform to their ideas just for the sake of it when I knew I should have been myself. Right now I think I would be very different if I hadn't been forced into things. I would be able to make independent judgments using my own intelligence. So let's not conform. Let's not be like other people so that each of us—great and good—can think and act for ourselves (17).

Another child viewed conformity in this way:

> In this day and age, I think people are trying to stress conformity too much. These people think that in our schools

everyone should develop the same habits and skills, be given the same amount of learning, all on the same subject. This kind of conformity can keep people from using their creativeness and ability to the fullest extent.

Conformity can cause other troubles. It gives you misconceptions of people. You judge a person by his group while the person might be entirely different from the group. I do not believe in doing what the guy before you did. I think everyone can think and create for himself. Our schools and churches and homes are stressing conformity today. If we could gather up enough courage to be ourselves instead of copying our neighbors, the world would be a lot happier place to live (13).

The conventional person does not develop his capacities, does not have an opportunity to realize what he can do. Cut off from his own desires, from his own being, he is not free to make choices based on a growing philosophy, on a developing meaning of life, and on existential value. He may appear to be a person with great sureness, with precise and emphatic ways of living, a confident person who takes possession of life. But, these are only attributes coordinated to the conventional views of success.

In the following poem (2, p. 49) Laotzu distinguishes the conventional man from the creative person:

Losing the way of life, men rely first on their fitness;
Losing fitness, they turn to kindness;
Losing kindness, they turn to justness;
Losing justness, they turn to convention.
Conventions are fealty and honesty gone to waste,
They are the entrance of disorder.
False teachers of life use flowery words
And start nonsense.
The man of stamina stays with the root
Below the tapering,
Stays with the fruit
Beyond the flowering:
He has his no and he has his yes.

I believe that much of the human misery in the world today, the serious emotional problems and conflicts, result from man's efforts to fit into conventional modes, from striving for goals of success, status, and power which provide no intrinsic value or satisfaction, and contribute to a meaningless existence. Failure to grow as a self results from a failure to maintain a unique identity in significant or crucial situations and an inability to meet others directly and honestly and with expressions of living love. Following traditional patterns and external guides, basing one's life on competitive striving and the rewards of the market place, modeling oneself after people in authority or with high status, the individual no longer knows who he is. He does not mean what he says and does not do what he believes and feels. Responding with surface or approved thoughts, he learns to use devious and indirect ways, and to base his behavior on the standards and expectations of others. He moves toward falsehood, fakery, pretense. His values and convictions do not emerge from real experience but derive from a feeling of danger and anxiety, from a fear of not keeping pace, a fear of being minimized, and a desire to be protected from rejection and attack. Cut off from his own self, he is unable to have honest experiences with others and communion with nature. His life is predicated on appearances, deceptions, and controlling behavior. Without any deep and growing roots, he moves in accordance with external signals. He does not know his place in the world, his position, where he is or who he is. He has lost touch with his own nature, his own spontaneity. He is unable to be a direct, genuine, loving human being.

To the degree that the individual strives to attain a similarity or congruity, to the degree that he acts in order to be popular, to be victorious, or to be approved of, and to the degree that he models himself after another person, he fails to emerge as a self, fails to develop his unique identity, fails to grow as a creative being consistent with his own desires and capacities and consistent with a life of genuine relatedness to others.

I have had the experience of living in a false world. One day I was deeply depressed by the severe criticisms a colleague had received—a person who was living his life in an honest and truthful sense, attempting to express his unique interests in his work. I felt especially saddened when I realized how he had suffered, when all he wanted to do was maintain a personal and creative identity, a genuine existence and relatedness. I felt especially sensitive to pretense and surface behavior, as though nothing were real. A numbness settled in, right at the center of my thought and feeling. That night even the children were unable to shake my grief and sadness. In their own spontaneous, unknowing ways, they tugged and pulled at me to draw me into life but for me there remained only suffering in the world.

After the children had gone to bed, I decided to go for a walk. The night was dark, filled with black clouds. Large white flakes of snow fell on and around me. The night was silent and serene. Suddenly, without understanding in any way, I experienced a transcendental beauty in the white darkness. It was difficult to walk on the glazed surface but as I walked I felt drawn to the black, inky streaks embedded in the ice. Dark, wavy lines, partly covered by snow, spread out in grotesque forms. I knelt down, touching the black, irregular patterns. Immediately I felt a chill but at the same time the ice began melting as my fingers touched it.

My inward heaviness lifted, and I was restored to a new capacity for exertion and endurance. I realized how, out of broken roots and fibers, in a genuine encounter with natural resources, it is possible to discover a new level of individual identity and to develop new strength and conviction. I realized how the self can be shattered in surface and false meetings when surrounded by intensive pressures to conform, and how in communion with nature the self can reach a new dimension of optimism and a new recognition of the creative way of life. Possibilities for unique and unusual meetings exist everywhere. We need only reach out in natural covering to come face to face with creation.

## REFERENCES

1. BUBER, MARTIN. *Hasidism and Modern Man.* Edited and translated by Maurice Friedman. New York: Horizon Press, 1958.
2. BYNNER, WITTER. *The Way of Life According to Laotzu.* An American Version. New York: The John Day Company, 1944.

3. CAMPH, DON. What Is Creative Ability? Clara Barton Junior High School, Royal Oak, Michigan, December, 1958.
4. CASSADY, JANIE. The Ability to Create. Clara Barton Junior High School, Royal Oak, Michigan, December, 1958.
5. CHANG, CHUNG-YUAN. Self-Realization and the Inner Process of Peace. *Main Currents in Modern Thought*, 15, 75-81.
6. CONNER, KAY. My Thoughts. Lockman School, Royal Oak, Michigan, March, 1959.
7. DELANEY, PAUL. The Wind. Lockman School, Royal Oak, Michigan, March, 1959.
8. GIBRAN, KAHLIL. *Sand and Foam*. New York: Alfred A. Knopf, 1926.
9. HORNEY, KAREN. Finding the Real Self. *Amer. J. Psychoanal.*, 9, 3-7, 1949.
10. KELMAN, HAROLD. Communing and Relating: Part III—Examples: General and Clinical. *Amer. J. Psychoanal.*, 19, 73-105, 1959.
11. KIERKEGAARD, SÖREN. *A Kierkegaard Anthology*. Edited by Robert Bretall. New Jersey: Princeton University Press, 1951.
12. MASLOW, A. H. Emotional Blocks to Creativity. *J. Individ. Psychol.*, 14, 51-56, 1958.
13. MCKITTRICK, RICKY. Concerning Conformity. Clara Barton Junior High School, Royal Oak, Michigan, December, 1958.
14. MILLER, RON. Creativity. Clara Barton Junior High School, Royal Oak, Michigan, December, 1958.
15. MOUSTAKAS, CLARK. Basic Approaches to Mental Health: A Human Relations Seminar of the Merrill-Palmer School. *J. Pers. and Guidance*, 37, 342-349, 1959.
16. MOUSTAKAS, CLARK. *Psychotherapy with Children: The Living Relationship*. New York: Harper and Bros., 1959.
17. OLESHANSKY, MARVIN. My Views on Conformity. Clara Barton Junior High School, Royal Oak, Michigan, December, 1958.
18. PARENT, SUSAN. How I Felt. Lockman School, Royal Oak, Michigan, March, 1959.
19. PETERSEN, JANET. The New Day. Clara Barton Junior High School, Royal Oak, Michigan, May, 1959.
20. REIK, THEODORE. *The Search Within*. New York: Farrar, Strauss and Cudahy, 1956.
21. RILKE, RAINER MARIA. *Letters to a Young Poet*. Translated by M. D. Herter Norton. Rev. ed. New York: W. W. Norton & Co., Inc., 1954.

22. SMITH, SANDRA. Spring. Lockman School, Royal Oak, Michigan, March, 1959.
23. WATTS, ALAN W. *Nature, Man, and Woman.* New York: Pantheon Books, Inc., 1958.
24. WILFONG, ROGER. When I Look Out the Window. Lockman School, Royal Oak, Michigan, March, 1959.
25. WILL, OTTO and COHEN, ROBERT H. A Report of a Recorded Interview in the Course of Psychotherapy. *Psychiat.*, 16, 263-282, 1953.

# 4

# Confrontation and Encounter

Only briefly are the deepest regions of the self ever known, yet within these brief encounters we come to know the value of love and communion. When we are in trouble, when we have made mistakes, when we are at odds with the world, when we have futile visions and dreams, caring for another person enables us to grow, to struggle with issues and problems, to carry out our hopes and aspirations.

Two ways in which the individual establishes significant bonds in his relations with others are the confrontation and the encounter. The confrontation is a meeting between persons who are involved in a conflict or controversy and who remain together, face-to-face, until their feelings of divisiveness and alienation are resolved. The encounter is a sudden, spontaneous, intuitive meeting with another person in which there is an immediate sense of relatedness, an immediate feeling of harmony and communion.

## THE CONFRONTATION

In our meetings with others conflicts arise and irritations grow until we no longer can continue to live with each other in the same way. Then, either the relationship will deteriorate or the persons will face each other and struggle with the issues and problems. The confrontation is not an intellectually planned session which requires an audience and a referee. It is a private, intimate conflict between persons which happens, often spontaneously and unexpectedly, when a crisis arises in a relationship and the persons must either reach a new level of life together or face the consequences of a broken relationship.

The confrontation may be brief or it may be of long

duration, depending on the depth and intensity of the dispute. It requires that the persons remain together until there is a resolution of feeling. The individuals may terminate the confrontation, still at odds as far as the issue is concerned, but not at odds with each other. This is the important point for everyone to realize—the other person must be free to maintain his own identity, to trust his own senses if a relationship is to have any valid meaning.

In the classroom confrontation, the child must have the right to be in disagreement with his teacher. Paradoxical as this seems, when persons can openly disagree, it is possible for them to establish genuine bonds. When the teacher forces the child to submit through repetitious phrases and commands, through conditioning, belittling, group pressures, brainwashing devices, or intimidation, the child soon realizes that the only acceptable way is the path of conformity. Increasingly, the child becomes insensitive to his own self and unresponsive to his own experience. He becomes numb to criticism and rebuke, develops a suspicious and mechanical defense against further attacks, and comes to be unfeeling in his associations with others.

Recently, I visited a second-grade classroom during a reading lesson. When the children saw the principal and me enter the room, they were eager to read to us. The teacher asked for volunteers. A child, with a smiling face and shining eyes, sitting next to me, was called on to read. She sighed with joy as she began, "Casey Joins the Circus." Apparently, she had learned that a good reader varies her tone of voice, reads loud enough for others to hear and reads fluently. Wanting to make an impression, wanting to get the praise of her teacher and classmates, she hurried through the paragraph assigned to her. But something was wrong. Mrs. Bell interrupted the child. She pushed the book away from the child's face and said in a slow deliberate voice, hovering over the child, "You are reading carelessly. That's not showing respect for what is printed on the page. It's not showing respect for our visitors or the other boys and girls. You are making sense but you simply are not reading the words in the book. I've told you about this before, Betsy.

Now you go back and read what's printed there so we can all follow you." The child returned to the beginning of the paragraph but something had happened. She had no direct, open way of responding. The staring, judging faces of the other children frightened her. She read in a reluctant manner, pronouncing words haltingly. There was a weak, muffled quality in her voice. She had been hurt. She was no longer certain. She completed the reading and slumped wearily into her chair.

The real tragedy was not in the critical words of the teacher or in the subdued child, but in the fact that no relationship between them existed. There was the teacher as law-giver and statement-maker, as the one in authority. There was the adult voice, belittling, shaming, humiliating the child into exact reading. The teacher used the visitors and the other children to prove her point and impress the child. She did not keep the issue between herself and the child, where it belonged. And it was all done matter-of-factly, as professional duty. It was all so impersonal and feelingless.

There was also the subdued, frightened voice of the child. The child read and she read and she read, every word in the paragraph. Was it worth killing that spontaneity, that joy, that wonder in a little girl's voice as she tried to please her audience, for the sake of a word-by-word conformity to a printed page?

This girl was not just a reader, not merely a machine producing and transmitting sounds. There beside me was a human being. She was really there, wanting to see her teacher smile, a gesture which would make her feel valued even though she made mistakes. But this teacher did not offer the child sympathy, respect, sensitivity, value. Instead, she performed a function. The confrontation never got beyond the initial reproof. Oh, yes, the child went through the motion of reading, but she was no longer there. She could not face her teacher as an open person any more.

No individual is perfect. We all make mistakes. But to commit a wrong, to lower the dignity of a child and not be aware that that dignity had been impaired, was much more serious than the child's skipping of words during oral reading. The real tragedy was the teacher's lack of sensitivity and awareness, her failure to recognize the child as a person.

When an adult loses sight of a child as a human being, when he fails to recognize the child's presence as a person, there is no reality between them, there is no relationship. This is what happens in many situations where potential growth and love exist between persons. The persons are lost when the discrepancy or issue becomes all that matters. The loudest voice, the strongest figure, the person in authority carries out his office of command. Gradually the child is forced into a state where feelings and senses are muffled and subdued until eventually he is no longer aware that he is experiencing them. When people reject, humiliate, hurt, belittle, control, dominate, and brutalize others without being aware of what they are doing, there is extreme danger that man will cease to be man.

Desensitization occurs through a process of deprivation and separation in which one is treated as an object; in which skills and subject matter are more significant than persons; in which goals must be pursued regardless of wishes, aspirations and capacities; in which rationalizing, explaining, and analyzing take the place of spontaneity and natural feeling. The adult who observes, manipulates and directs a child, probes him, writes him up, and breaks him down into specific traits of weakness and strength is actually treating him as a thing—and the child soon learns to react as one. When a child is perceived as an object, when he is treated as a member of a group or mass society, without reference to his unique and varying differences, there is real danger that he will lose his own identity as a growing person. Building a wall around himself for protection against the penalties of being honest and forthright, he will become insensitive to laughter and mimicry and sarcasm, and also insensitive to the range of feelings that characterize genuine human existence.

In its extreme form, what happens in everyday life to encourage dehumanization is not unlike what occurred in the death camps during World War II. The dehumanization of the prisoner of war is forcefully described by

Viktor Frankl (5, pp. 19-20) in this brief narrative based on his experiences in four concentration camps:

> At first the prisoner looked away if he saw the punishment parades of another group; he could not bear to see fellow prisoners march up and down for hours in the mire, their movements directed by blows. Days or weeks later things changed. The prisoner did not avert his eyes any more. By then his feelings were blunted, and he watched unmoved. He stood unmoved while a twelve-year-old boy was carried in who had been forced to stand at attention for hours in the snow or to work outside with bare feet because there were no shoes for him in the camp. His toes had become frostbitten, and the doctor on duty picked off the black gangrenous stumps with tweezers, one by one. Disgust, horror and pity are emotions that our spectator could not really feel any more. The sufferers, the dying and the dead, became such commonplace sights to him after a few weeks of camp life that they could not move him any more.

The rise of existentialism and Zen Buddhism, both of which are concerned with the unique, humanness of man, is a protest against the dangers of conformity and dehumanization which now threaten modern societies. Norman Cousins (4) has registered this editorial warning:

> What is happening, I believe, is that the natural reactions of the individual against violence are being blunted. The individual is being desensitized by living history. He is developing new reflexes and new responses that tend to slow up the moral imagination and relieve him of essential indignation over impersonal hurt. He is becoming casual about brutality. He makes his adjustments to the commonplace, and nothing is more commonplace in our age than the ease with which life can be smashed or shattered. The range of the violence sweeps from the personal to the impersonal, from the amusements of the crowd to the policies of nations. It is in the air, quite literally. It has lost the sting of surprise.
>
> The desensitization of twentieth-century man is more than a danger to the common safety. It represents the loss or impairment of the noblest faculty of human life—the ability to be aware both of suffering and beauty; the ability to share sorrow and create hope; the ability to think and respond beyond one's wants. There are some things we have no right ever to get used to. One of these most certainly is brutality.

The other is the irrational. Both brutality and the irrational have now come together and are moving towards a dominant pattern. If the pattern is to be resisted and changed, a special effort must be made. A very special effort.

In contrast to the confrontation which does not get beyond the initial issue or conflict, is the relationship between two persons where, for example, the adult faces the child with his misdemeanor but remains with him and enables him to come to terms with his own immorality, wrong-doing, or irresponsibility. In a true confrontation the persons always remain persons. And because there is awareness and knowledge and sensitivity, the argument, the face-to-face struggle, follows its natural course and opens new pathways of relatedness. In times of creative confrontation, the relationship unfolds into more and more meaningful expressions of the self. Feelings are released, conflicts resolved and a new sense of responsibility developed. In a real meeting, the adult is present as a whole person engaged in a life with the child in which all dimensions and resources of the self converge, in which the whole being comes to grips with an impelling human conflict.

The confrontation is a means to a significant life between persons, but each must maintain an awareness of his feelings and must be honest enough and courageous enough to let the initial breach heal.

In the creative disputation, each person must be aware of the other's full legitimacy. Neither must lose sight of the fact that he is seeking in his own way, with whatever talents and skills he possesses, to find some meaningful way to live, to express the truth as he sees it. In no way is either person reduced by this.

In the classroom, the teacher has an additional challenge and responsibility. The conflict with a pupil can be the supreme test for the educator, who must face this conflict and come through it to a meaningful way of life, a life where confidence continues unshaken, even strengthened. In his essay on the education of character, Buber (1, pp. 107-108) describes the difficulty of creative resolution of conflict between teacher and child, as illustrated in this passage:

> He must use his own insight wholeheartedly; he must not blunt the piercing impact of his knowledge, but he must at the same time have in readiness the healing ointment for the heart pierced by it. Not for a moment may he conduct a dialectical maneuver instead of the real battle for truth. But if he is the victor he has to help the vanquished endure defeat; and if he cannot conquer the self-willed soul that faces him (for victories over souls are not so easily won), then he has to find the word of love which alone can help to overcome so difficult a situation.

The adult is sometimes afraid to confront a child who is hostile, caustic, or vengeful. Such an adult avoids him until the accumulation of feelings becomes so unbearable that an explosion occurs and the adult loses control. Once the self is out of control, there is no possibility to bring about a positive resolution of the problem. But when the hateful, rejecting emotions subside, there is always hope that the adult can come to terms with the child and reach a depth of relatedness and mutuality. The anxiety in facing an embittered, destructive child can be eliminated only by an actual confrontation with the dreaded creature because until we actually meet him, we cannot know him. We cannot know whether we can live with him, or whether we can face the issue and maintain our own identity with love.

Viewing the child solely as an immature person is a way of escaping confronting him. Thinking of him only as a learner who is slow or lazy or careless is a way of avoiding the feelings a controversial meeting may bring forth. Considering him as the "other" is all part of the estrangement process, when professional and social roles separate and alienate adult and child as persons.

In the true confrontation, the external, objective framework is abandoned. The individual departs from the familiar and goes forth to an unknown meeting with the other person. The threat of anxiety to some extent can be controlled by avoiding the unknown, by restricting the scope of life, by remaining immersed in the familiar and not venturing out. Because this makes for stagnation and constriction, we must determine to go forward to keep open the doors to an expanding life with others (9, p. 45).

*Brian* (8, pp. 17-20)

Something in the nature of anxiety in confronting an enraged child who has broken a limit in therapy held me for many years. Until recently I rationalized and explained away my anxiety to the point of convincing myself that to end the interview was the appropriate response to the repeated breaking of a limit. This used to be my way of teaching the child his responsibility to the relationship. After many such experiences, I realized, however, that I had never lived with an enraged child long enough to know what it actually means to be with a child who refuses to be denied. I had sent the child away at a time when love and understanding mattered most to him.

I realized one day with Brian that I had some growing to do, that I had to see what existed beyond my fixed policy of terminating a meeting when it became disorganized and destructive. I saw that if a child broke a limit, I could set another one and another. I saw that I could, without jeopardizing the value of consistency and strength in a relationship, remain with a child in severe conflict until bedrock was reached; until an ultimate limit, a true dimension of the unfolding relationship, could be established and held. Then the relationship could grow while the child faced his fear and anger. When the adult holds steadfast in the relationship and keeps the reality between himself and the child alive, the possibility exists for discovery of new insights, meaningful roots, and positive development.

Brian had been coming for weekly therapy sessions for almost a year when his intense feelings of love and hate reached a peak. For three months, each experience had begun with a sword and gun battle between us. He screamed with delight each time he "pierced or cut" me, each time he shot and killed me. When these battles were first initiated we had agreed to keep them within a ten-minute time limit. Following the battle with me, he would proceed to shoot and kill all human and animal figures in the room. He would take a rifle and scrape to the floor all items on tables and the tops of cabinets. Often he would open the plastic paint containers and place them at the edge of a shelf, shooting at them until the paint sprayed against the walls and onto the floor. This barrage and the hostile attack had been repeated in similar pattern for thirteen weeks. Then one day we faced each other on a different interpersonal level.

The usual ten-minute battle had been completed but Brian refused to stop. He decided to use me as a target for what he called "bow and arrow" practice. I explained that there were items in the room that he could use for practice but that I did not wish to be his target. The following conversation took place:

MR. M: Brian, I have already explained I do not want to be used as a target. (*As I express my feeling, Brian shoots again, this time hitting my arm.*)

MR. M: Brian, that hurt. Perhaps that's what you want—to hurt me. (*Brian is about to shoot again.*)

MR. M: No, Brian. I will not permit it again. I'm going to have to insist that you give me the bow and arrows. I do not intend to let you shoot me again. (*Brian laughs nervously. With a sadistic glee in his voice, he tries to pull away but I hold the bow firmly. He drops the arrows.*)

MR. M: I'll just put these out of reach for the rest of this hour. You can play with them again next time you come. (*Brian throws the bow at me. I pick it up and remove it. He picks up a pistol, gun belt, and knife and throws them at me with much force. I go over to him and hold his arms.*)

MR. M: I can see nothing will satisfy you until you've hurt me. You're determined to have it your way, but I'm just as determined not to be a target for your attacks. If you persist I'm going to have to make all these things out of bounds for the rest of the time. (*Brian laughs in my face as I talk to him. He pulls away.*)

BRIAN: You never let me do anything. All you ever think of is No! No! No!

MR. M: Yes, I know. You think I stop you at every turn.

BRIAN: (*Throws a container of paint at me.*) I hate you.

MR. M: You have every right to hate me but I will not permit you to throw things at me. For the rest of this time this entire section of the playroom is out of bounds. (*Brian is infuriated. He glares angrily at me. His eyes focus on the blackboard, a cunning look crosses his face, and a sneering smile.*)

BRIAN: Will you play tic-tac-toe with me?

MR. M: Yes, if you'd like me to, but I saw your thought.

I know what you intend doing. If you throw one more item at me I'm going to have to do something drastic. (*The game begins. Suddenly Brian begins laughing wildly. He throws the chalk and eraser at me. He tries to run to the "out-of-bounds" area. I block his path. He picks up a pile of books and throws them.*)

MR. M: All right, Brian. Everything in the room is out of bounds for the rest of this time. You may have only this small space here. We can sit and talk or just sit.

BRIAN: You can't make me stay in this part.

MR. M: Oh, yes, I can. We've reached a point now where this is the only place we have. (*Pause.*)

BRIAN: I hate you. (*Pause.*) I could kill you.

MR. M: Yes, you really want to hurt me the way you feel I have hurt you. (*Brian slaps me.*)

MR. M: I now must hold your arms. (*Suddenly Brian completely relaxes. He lays his head on my shoulder.*)

BRIAN: You never let the baby have his bottle.

MR. M: You always had to cry and throw things before you were fed.

BRIAN: I want my bottle.

MR. M: Would you like me to rock you? (*Sitting together quietly on the floor, the therapist rocks Brian a few minutes. Brian becomes tense again.*)

BRIAN: I hate you. I could kill you. (*Brian begins spitting, I turn him around.*)

MR. M: It's as hard for me to have to hold you as it is for you to be held. I know you are doing what you feel you must, but we have reached a point now where I am also doing what I feel I must. (*Brian screams and laughs shrilly.*)

MR. M: It's time to leave now, Brian. Do you want to walk out by yourself or do you want me to take you out?

BRIAN: I'll go myself. (*Brian walks toward the door. As he reaches it, he picks up several items and throws them at me. He comes toward me and pushes and punches at me. I take him and pull him out the door.*)

MR. M: I realize, Brian, you couldn't hold to your decision. It's all right. (*Brian begins to cry silently.*)

BRIAN: I hate you and I never want to see you again.

MR. M: But I want to see you again. I'll be here at the same time next week. (*Brian leaves.*)

This was a full, vital, complete experience of two persons, involving struggle, suffering, and pain—but it was also a growth experience. The limits were important not only because they provided a structure in which self-exploration could occur, but also because they emerged as necessary within a situation where child and therapist faced each other as whole beings and lived through the significant controversy. Eventually Brian and I formed deep ties between us and the roots of a healthy relationship.

The dispute over the broken limit significantly affected the outcome of psychotherapy. When Brian returned, he greeted me with a feeling of intimacy and relatedness. He plunged into new areas of conflict and emotionalized expression. Having lived through a significant controversy with his therapist, having met him as a person, Brian was able to verbalize his feelings of self-doubt, to say that his parents considered him a "bad," destructive child, and to relate directly a number of crucial experiences in which he had been severely denied as a self. Thus, in spite of the apparent breach, child and therapist formed deep ties between themselves which enabled the child to develop a sense of self and the freedom of real self-expression.

I conclude this section with a confrontation involving a strong disagreement between a teacher and a class of eighth grade children. The situation is narrated by the teacher herself.

### *Mrs. Lawrence Confronts Her Group*

Over a period of many months, a fairly successful teacher-indoctrination or "brainwashing" had been executed in this group on the joys of research study and the woeful disadvantages of using just one textbook for their work. But, someplace along the line another job of "thinking and speaking for yourself, expressing your own convictions" had been running a strong counter course! Like a regiment in ambush they sprang one quiet day; almost united to a man on the pleasure they would derive from having a text, a single book, with discussion questions and problem exercises, "like the other kids." Being kicked in the stomach might have been less painful to me at that moment; and to save the sinking ship and the drowning crew, I pulled out all the stops.

"Have you no appreciation of the value of looking at things more than one way? Can't you see the *fun* you could have putting ideas together from many phases of American life and from many different sources? What about the legends, literature, art, music, and dances of your people," I stormed. "Can't you draw some conclusions of your own? Must you have it crammed down your throats from the pages of one little book; and one dictating teacher." And for a final "piece de resistance", in words to this effect, or more accurately, in these very words, I said, "You are all just plain lazy! You want to be spoon fed."

Well, there was hardly a dry eye in the house, the little scene I had staged had brought about the desired effect! Proud? Well, at that moment perhaps, but still rational enough to add; "You needn't decide now what you want to do; but tomorrow I will expect you to indicate on a slip of paper if you prefer to have the textbook for the year, or if you would prefer to work together from many resources and research methods toward some meaningful insights and conclusions."

When my shaking stopped, and I sat in my empty classroom, I began thinking of the ugliness of the whole thing! This is teaching? Victory at any cost? It didn't take too long for me to realize that some of the very people who mattered most must now wonder if they really know me as an honest self. Where was the consistency of my values now?

I can't honestly say that I knew what I was going to do about it when I walked in to class the next day; in spite of the long night's struggle and post-mortem of the confrontation, but I applied, through no advanced plan of my own, the age old principle of apologizing when you know you have done something wrong. I held to my belief in the value of the resources, methods and principles we had used in the past months, but I admitted temporary irrationalism and professed that my lack of respect for their opinions was inexcusable! If it would afford them a better opportunity to state their views, and if it wasn't too late, I suggested a discussion. Everyone had something to say and the cleansing power of my words resulted in a completely different classroom atmosphere and a heightened sense of group solidarity. My pleasure in being a part of this was only commensurate with the knowledge that I had learned far more than any child in the room from this experience.

## THE ENCOUNTER

The encounter is a direct meeting between two persons who happen to come together. It may be an exchange of brief duration or last a long time, a meeting with a friend or a total stranger. In such a meeting there is human intimacy and depth. Although every confrontation is an encounter, not every encounter involves a dispute or controversy. Sometimes the encounter is a simple coming together of two faces or pairs of eyes, a sudden sense of knowing and being within the other, a feeling of harmony. The encounter is an immediate, imminent reality between two persons engaged in a living communion, where there is an absolute relatedness and a sense of mutuality.

The encounter is a creative experience, in which there is a dropping off of conventions, a letting go, so that one enters into the reality of a situation in terms of the conditions and requirements intrinsic to that situation. Openness, receptiveness, and relatedness are significant aspects of the encounter. There is a free and open play of attention, thought, feeling, and perception. The openness and intensity of interest may range from the grave, the serious, the absorbing, and the tantalizing to the playful and fleeting (9, p. 242).

The encounter is not a fortuitous meeting of two individuals, but rather a decisive inner experience in which something totally new is revealed, in which new horizons are opened (6, p. 119). Martin Buber (1 pp. 112-113) relates an encounter between an educator and a student, a vital meeting which occurred when a young teacher faced his class for the first time.

Undecided whether to issue orders immediately or to set up rules and standards of conduct, the teacher suddenly encounters a face in the crowd, a face which impresses him. It is not a beautiful face, but a real face and it contains an expression into which the teacher reads the question: "Who are you? Do you know something that concerns me?" I quote the passage that presents this encounter:

> In some such way he reads the question. And he, the young teacher, addresses this face. He says nothing very ponderous or important, he puts an ordinary introductory question: "What did you talk about last in geography? The Dead Sea? Well, what about the Dead Sea?" But there was obviously something not quite usual in the question, for the

answer he gets is not the ordinary schoolboy answer; the boy begins *to tell a story*. Some months earlier he had stayed for a few hours on the shores of the Dead Sea and it is of this he tells. He adds: "Everything looked to me as if it had been created a day before the rest of creation." Quite unmistakably he had only in this moment made up his mind to talk about it. In the meantime his face has changed. It is no longer quite as chaotic as before. And the class has fallen silent. They all listen. The class, too, is no longer a chaos. Something has happened. The young teacher has started from above.

No matter how complicated or restricted or frightening life appears to be, the opportunity for encounter is always present. However heavy the pressures and responsibilities of life, there is nothing that can completely prevent genuine meetings with other persons. The possibility of encounter exists as a reality if a person is willing to make the required human commitment.

My own relationship with adults was significantly altered through an experience with an old man—particularly my capacity to bear pain and suffering, and my sensitivity to loneliness. This encounter involved one person who hated himself and wanted to die and another person who desired to live with him during the most devastating illness of his life.

*Communal Loneliness* (7, pp. 20-23)

He stood in the doorway of my office, a terribly stooped old man, pain and misery, heavy wrinkles, lined his face. He stared beyond me, fiery, piercing eyes fixed to the floor, a face filled with indescribable loneliness and defeat. "Won't you come in and sit down?" I asked gently. He entered the room, but he did not sit. He began to pace, back and forth, back and forth. Increasingly, I felt the turbulence inside him which electrified my office with a kind of frozen tension. The tension mounted, becoming almost unbearable. Heavy beads of perspiration fell from his forehead and face. Tears filled his eyes. He started to speak several times but the words would not come. He stroked his hair roughly and pulled at his clothing. The pacing continued.

I felt his suffering keenly, deep inside me, spreading throughout my whole body. I remarked, "So utterly painful and lonely." "Lonely," he cried. "Lonely!" "Lonely!" he shouted, "I've been alone all my life." He spoke in rasping tones, his nerves drawn taut. "I've never been an honest person. I've never done anything I really wanted to do, nothing I truly believed in. I don't know what I believe in any more. I don't know what I feel. I don't know what to do with myself. I wish I could die—how I have yearned, how I have longed for death to come, to end this misery. If I had the courage, I would kill myself. These headaches. Have you ever known such lasting pain? I don't know how much more I can stand. I haven't slept for months. I wake up in the middle of the night. Everything is dark, black, ugly, empty. Right now my head is throbbing. I take pills. I try to rest. I avoid becoming upset. Nothing helps. My head is splitting. I don't think I can take this pain much longer. I wake with a start. My heart fills with terror. My wife and children are asleep, with me in the house—but I am entirely alone. I am not a father. I am not a husband. I'm no one. Look! See these tears? I could weep forever. Forever. I sometimes feel I cry for the whole world—a world that's sour and lost."

All this the old man uttered—sobbing, choking, sighing, gasping for breath. The sounds were thick. His tongue was fastened to his gums. Only with the greatest effort did he talk. It was almost unendurable. The lancinating physical pain and mental anguish mounted relentlessly. There was not even a moment of suspension so we could breathe normally and recapture our resources. His distress was cumulative, increasingly exhaustive.

In his completely weakened state, unknown urges, unknown capacities, a surprising strength enabled him to continue. From the beginning he had never been a real person. It was too late now, he felt. Nothing in life was real. For seventy-four years he had lived by other people's descriptions of him, others' perceptions of him. He had come to believe that this was his real self. He had become timid and shy, when he might have discovered and developed social interests. He was silent when he might have something to say. He played cards every Tuesday and attended club meetings every Thursday when he might have enjoyed being alone, or conversing with his wife, or developing an avocation or hobby. He listened to the radio and watched television every evening when he might have discovered values in music and books. He did not know his real interests and talents, his real aspirations and goals. He never gave himself time to discover himself.

He asked in agony, "Do you know what it means not to feel anything, to be completely without feeling? Do you understand what it is to know only pain and loneliness? My family doesn't understand me. They think I have these headaches because my business is failing. They think I roam the house at night, moving from bed to couch to chair to floor, because I'm worrying about my business. They think I'm worrying about new possibilities and plans. So they soften me and treat me gingerly. Husband and father must have a quiet house, so the house is quiet. I must not be upset, so I am avoided. I must not be expected to be friendly and sociable because I am passive and shy. I must be indirectly talked into doing what they want, in the right way, at the right moment. It takes careful planning. I must have sympathy, even if it's false, to be able to face the tough, competitive world outside. They cannot and will not recognize that this man they handle with kid gloves, whom they fear upsetting, whom they decide has to be coddled and manipulated into buying new clothes, a new car, a new home, all the other possessions a family feels it must have, this man does not really exist and never did. But who am I? I do not know and I do not know how to find out. Can't you see? I do not really exist. I am nothing. Do you know what it is not to know how you feel, not to know your own thoughts, not to know what you believe, not to know what you want, not to be sure of anything but endless pain and suffering? And everyone else takes you for granted, on already formed opinions and actions, the same words, the same ways. How do I start to live again? I'm dying and I can't stop breathing. I can't stop living."

These were the themes of our talks together—self-denial, estrangement, rejection, pain, spreading loneliness. We met eight times. In each visit, his suffering and sense of isolation increased, reaching unbelievable heights. Often, I thought: "Surely this is it. He has reached the breaking point." He seemed at the very end of his power and resources. But he kept coming until I wondered whether I had not reached the breaking point. The only thing that kept me going was the certainty that without me there would be no one—no one at all. I could not abandon him, even when I questioned my own strength to continue to live through our conversations and the lonely terror not expressible in words. I suffered deeply in these hours with him. Each time he came I felt on the verge of sinking into total despair. Often when he wept, there were tears in my eyes too, and when his head ached painfully, I felt the pain all the way through me. And when he paced and pulled at himself, I felt a terrible restlessness and agitation. And when he was utterly alone and lonely, I was alone and lonely too. My full, complete presence was not enough to alleviate his suffering, his self-lacerating expressions. I felt an awful loneliness and desolation as I was not able to help him find a beginning, locate a direction, discover a new pathway of relatedness to himself and others. It hurt me deeply to see him grow increasingly, unbelievably tortured and not be able to help him find a meaning or even some beginning belief in the possibility of a good life. He was dying before me and something within me was dying too. I could not reach him. I do not know what effort of will power, what inner strivings of the heart, what forces kept me going in the face of this unendurable, mounting desolation, despair, and loneliness. I felt defeated and weakened, yet each time he came I met him squarely, honestly, directly. Each time my capacity for bearing with him seemed to be reaching a terminal point, new threads inside revived me. Somehow fresh strength flowed into me, mysteriously encouraging me and enabling me to continue. I listened to him and believed in him. I was convinced he had the power within himself to find a new meaning in life. I continued to live with him in the crucial hours of psychic dying. My entire office filled with his aching. I could feel it everywhere in the room—in the floor, the walls, the furniture, the papers and books on my desk. It settled irrevocably and held stationary. For some time after he left, I did not move. I remained heavy as the feeling he left when he departed.

Then on the ninth appointment he did not come. What could this defection mean? How had I failed? Had he sensed my own growing struggle, my own exhaustion, my own loneliness? I searched within my self and within our relationship but I could find no satisfactory answer.

Two weeks passed before he called. He spoke in a calm voice, in a totally different way from any previous words. "It's all so fresh and raw," he said, "and so new and startling that I'm constantly uncertain, but I feel I am coming into a totally new existence. I sometimes doubt that what I'm feeling will last, but the feelings have persisted now almost two weeks and I'm beginning to recognize them as my own. I do not know what is happening or how, but by some strange miracle or inner working, I am beginning to breathe again and to live again. I do not want to see you just now because I must have further confirmation, but I will call you soon."

Six weeks later the old man came for the last time. I could barely recognize him. He looked youthful. His face was alive. His smile was radiant and so thrilling I felt tingling sensations everywhere inside me. He spoke warmly, confidently, "I came only to see your face light up, to be warmed by the gleam in your eyes. I know how much you suffered. I have seen your tortured face even after leaving you. I'll just sit here with you quietly a few minutes." So we sat in silence, each reveling in the birth, each warmed by a bond that emerged from deep and spreading roots in the hours of anguish and loneliness. We were no longer alone or lonely. We had found a new strength and sustenance in each other.

The fundamental communion in which we suffered enabled him to get to the very depths of his experience. Perhaps in arriving at the foundation of his grief and loneliness, immediate death or immediate life were the only choices within reach. He chose to live. From his rock bottom loneliness emerged a new life and a real self was restored.

Martin Buber expresses this feeling in the following passage from *Hasidism and Modern Man* (2, pp. 120-121):

> . . . not to help out of pity, that is, out of a sharp, quick pain which one wishes to expel, but out of love, that is, out of living with the other. He who pities does not live with the suffering of the sufferer, he does not bear it in his heart as one bears the life of a tree with all its drinking in and shooting forth and with the dream of its roots and the craving of its trunk and the thousand journeys of its branches, or as one bears the life of an animal with all its gliding, stretching, and grasping and all the joy of its sinews and its joints and the dull tension of its brain. He does not bear in his heart this special essence, the suffering of the other; rather he receives from the most external features of this suffering a sharp, quick pain, unbridgeably dissimilar to the original pain of the sufferer. And it is thus that he is moved. But the helper must live with the other, and only help that arises out of living with the other can stand before the eyes of God.

## REFERENCES

1. BUBER, MARTIN. *Between Man and Man.* London: Routledge and Kegan Paul Ltd., 1947.
2. BUBER, MARTIN. *Hasidism and Modern Man.* New York: Horizon Press, 1958.

3. BUBER, MARTIN. *I and Thou.* Edinburgh, Scotland: T. & T. Clark, 1937.
4. COUSINS, NORMAN. The Desensitization of Twentieth-Century Man. *Saturday Review*, May 16, 1959.
5. FRANKL, VIKTOR E. *Man's Search for Meaning: An Introduction to Logo Therapy*. Boston: Beacon Press, 1962.
6. MAY, ROLLO; ANGEL, ERNEST; ELLENBERGER, HENRI F. (Editors). *Existence: A New Dimension in Psychiatry and Psychology*. New York: Basic Books, 1958.
7. MOUSTAKAS, CLARK E. *Loneliness*. Englewood Cliffs, N.J.: Prentice-Hall, Inc., 1961.
8. MOUSTAKAS, CLARK E. *Psychotherapy with Children: The Living Relationship*. New York: Harper & Brothers, 1959.
9. SCHACHTEL, ERNEST G. *Metamorphosis*. New York: Basic Books, 1959.
10. SUZUKI, D. T.; FROMM, ERICH; DEMARTINO, RICHARD. *Zen Buddhism and Psychoanalysis*. New York: Harper & Brothers, 1960.

# 5

# Honesty, Idiocy, and Manipulation

When I meet another person as a full human self, I meet him in the realm of the intangible. In each of us there is a substance which makes possible a sense of continuity, commitment, and mutuality. This unifying substance enables the individual to experience a feeling of wholeness and a particular identity.

The adhesive nature of the self appropriates its character through honest self-expression. When I am honest, there is an uncompromising commitment to an authentic existence, in a particular moment of experience. No other moment matters but the moment in which I am living and no other existence matters but that which is alive and present in me at this moment of life. Honesty of self unites the self and provides the active moral sense which governs one's actions.

I am honest when my experience is consistent with my real feelings, perceptions, and senses, even when these depart sharply from the experience of others. If twelve people viewing a scene observe that there are eight trees but I see only a pattern of light and color and movement, I claim a configuration, even though all the others see eight trees. It is the integrating meaning in perception that determines the nature of individual reality, and not the number of objects or traits tabulated by a machine or observed in a detached manner.

I am speaking of the kind of self-experience that is decisively different from the objective view, from that of the onlooker and observer who exist separated from that which they perceive. Buber explains this difference as follows:

> Consequently what they experience in this way, whether it is, as with the observer, a sum of traits, or, as with the onlooker, an existence, neither demands action from them

> nor inflicts destiny on them. . . . it is a different matter when in a receptive hour of my personal life a man meets me about whom there is something, which I cannot grasp in any objective way at all, that "says something" to me. That does not mean, says to me what manner of man this is, what is going on in him, and the like. But it means, says something to me, addresses something to me, speaks something that enters my own life (1, pp. 8-9).

Genuine development of the self requires honesty of expression, creating meanings from one's own real experiences, and taking a definite position consistent with these experiences. Honesty implies a willingness to assert what one sees and an allegiance to what one perceives. Being true to one's own experience is the central requirement in the continued existence of a real self. Every distortion of experience creates a false self, pulling the person in a direction which is less than whole, and forcing upon the self fragments of life, the eyes of another, the heart of another, the soul of another.

However imperfect one's senses may be, a person can feel, touch, hear, taste, only that which he experiences himself. The self is incapable of being false to this trust; it cannot be deceived. Honesty is required; simple, open, direct honesty is the only way to wholeness, unity, and authenticity of existence.

The lie gnaws at the center of being, blocks spontaneity, and destroys the integrative quality of the self. The lie is the beginning of a process which leads to self-deception and self-negation. The dynamics involved in this process are quoted by John Shlien from Jean-Paul Sartre's study of schizophrenia:

> The liar, for one thing, is in possession of the truth. He sees both sides. He intends to deceive, and does not hide his intention from himself. . . . It "happens often enough that the liar is more or less the victim of it, that he half persuades himself of it." There's the rub, there's the treachery of it. The lie ("I could not have done that," "It never happened," etc.) begun in self-defense slips into self-deception (7, p. 297).

Shlien continues this discussion of the underlying dynamics of the lie:

If the one who lies is the same as the one to whom the lie is told, then he must know, in his capacity as deceiver, the truth which is hidden from him as the one deceived. Must know it well in order to conceal it, but this requires a duality which has been lost, so he can neither know certainly nor conceal cynically, nor affirm his being by negation of the "other." There is not virtue in the lie. There is a purpose in understanding it, and its relationship to the truth at one pole and to self-deception at the opposite pole, that is, to throw some light on the dynamism of a "defense mechanism" as it leads to self-destruction and essential loss of being . . . (7, pp. 297-300).

Being honest in a relationship is at times exceedingly difficult and painful. Yet the moment a person evades the truth, central fibres of the self pull away, and he initiates a process of deception. Ultimately, deviation from the truth is a form of manipulation, a form of power over the other person or a destructive control of oneself. Evasion, self-denial, and distortion are usually motivated by a wish to influence, change, and direct. Even when fear motivates distortion, the fear is a way of manipulating the other person by preventing him from discovering one's own real thoughts or feelings. If I did not manipulate the person would I not be as I am? Would I remain silent by deliberate and calculated control when my beliefs, my convictions, my feelings urge expression?

Conflicts originate between men when they do not say what they mean and do not do what they say. Dishonesty in man's relationship to man leads to profound and inevitable destruction. Buber asserts, "For this construes and poisons, again and again and in increasing measure, the situation between myself and the other man, and I, in my internal disintegration, am no longer able to master it but, contrary to all my illusions, have become its slave. By our contradiction, our lie, we foster conflict-situations and give them power over us until they enslave us. From here, there is no way out but by the crucial realization: Everything depends on myself; and the crucial decision: I will straighten myself out" (2, p. 158).

When I speak of truth and honesty I do not necessarily mean boldly outspoken beliefs stated aggressively and without reserve. Nor do I mean the conscious, thought-out, calculated statements intended to provoke and foment, although honesty may sometimes take these forms. I do not mean honesty which is hostile and destructive, which hurts or minimizes or destroys. I do not mean the aggressive thrust or challenge which aims to attack. I do not mean the "holier than thou" attitude which limits and restricts. All of these are perversions of a simple truth, a truth which exists solely because it is a vital piece of self-experience. Honesty, as I know it, means the quiet, direct expressions which sometimes emerge reluctantly, hesitantly and even fearfully. It refers only to the self of the person, the person's own search for truth, not to the presence or absence of honesty in anyone else. My task in honesty is to maintain an allegiance to my own self, not to hurl catchwords and pet phrases at others.

Rarely is honesty the best policy from the standpoint of freedom from suffering or achievement of material gain. In a competitive society where status, economic prestige, and power are highly prized, the honest person is considered naive, immature, and child-like because he destroys his own chances for success and accomplishment. Failure of the honest person to achieve respect and happiness is painfully related in Dostoevski's brilliant novel, *The Idiot*. Myshkin's fate, as an honest and kind man in a society more concerned with wealth, power and conquest than with humanistic ideals, was that of evoking as much distrust as love. Eventually he was defeated and destroyed by a corrupt and dissipated society.

The honest person, trying to live simply, directly, and openly is often regarded with suspicion and imputed to have evil and hidden motives. Let us examine the way in which some of the characters in *The Idiot* viewed Myshkin. First of all, there was the servant in the Epanchin household who became suspicious when Myshkin answered his questions directly and honestly. Myshkin did not play the role of the visitor, presenting a noble or "class" face, but rather he spoke to the servant as an equal, in a way perfectly suitable from man to man but utterly inappropriate from a visitor to a manservant. The servant, overcome with distrust, thought Myshkin was either an impostor or a man soft in the head and devoid of his wits and his dignity (3, p. 18). Consider today how much more diverse, complicated, and delineated are the roles undertaken and the games played; how little spontaneity is encouraged and how lengthy the rules and policies governing who speaks to whom, in what way, at what time, and under what conditions. A lineally oriented society (5) based on conventions and standards and roles breeds deception and mask-like behavior.

Continuing with the attitudes of distrust and suspicion expressed against Myshkin, Aglaia, who loved him, doubted his veracity, exclaiming, ". . . it's horrid of him to play a part. Is he trying to gain something by it?" (3, p. 52). Ganya, who was also deeply suspicious of Myshkin, caused him great anguish and treated him as deceitful and devious. In a moving confrontation, bewildered by the fact that Myshkin has completely gained the love and confidence of the Epanchin family in a brief period of time, Ganya faces Myshkin in a state of violent agitation and disbelief:

> "And she gave it you—gave it you herself to read? Herself?"
>
> "Yes; and I assure you I shouldn't have read it unless she asked me to."
>
> Ganya was silent for a minute, reflecting with painful effort. But suddenly he cried:
>
> "Impossible! She couldn't have told you to read it. You are lying! You read it of yourself."
>
> "I am speaking the truth," answered Myshkin in the same perfectly untroubled voice, "and I assure you I am very sorry that it is so distasteful to you" (3, p. 82).

Doubt and suspicion are often aroused in the presence of truth and honesty. What lies beneath this man's simplicity? What devious and cunning scheme is being perpetrated? What does he wish to gain? These attitudes were expressed again and again in Myshkin's meetings with others.

Ivan Fyodorovitch remarks to him, "One wouldn't have thought you were that sort of fellow. Why, I looked on you as a philosopher. Ah, the sly dog!" (3, p. 135).

When Myshkin says to Ferdyshtchenko, "I've made you no confession. I simply answered your question." Ferdyshtchenko shouts, "Bravo! Bravo! That's sincere anyway—it's sly and sincere too" (3, p. 135).

Then there is the analysis of Myshkin's honesty (or idiocy) as an exploitative and selfish condition. Lebedyev's nephew puts it this way: "Yes, prince, one must do you justice, you do know how to make use of your . . . well, illness (to express it politely); you've managed to offer your friendship and money in such an ingenious way that now it's impossible for an honourable man to take it under any circumstances. That's either a bit too innocent or a bit too clever . . . You know best which" (3, p. 273).

Again and again, Myshkin is charged with ulterior motives. Even his most direct, open and straightforward words are misunderstood and misjudged. He is treated as a curiosity and as a simpleton, with the word "idiot" frequently uttered behind his back. And so to most of us, the honest man is a riddle. What is he after? What is in it for him? What is behind the simplicity? What is he trying to get me to do or believe?

A person may speak honestly and sincerely, may answer a question in the light of what exists as meaningful for him. He may speak centrally and at the very heart of his subject and still not be valued, but rather teased, belittled, and laughed at because he speaks of an experience which is peculiar, unusual, unconventional, or unpopular. To illustrate this point, I would like to quote at length an incident from *The Idiot*. Myshkin is surrounded by Madame Epanchin and her three daughters who have beseeched him to tell them something of his experience, something important in his personal development. Myshkin, referring to his epileptic seizures and the period following his recovery, tells the women that after his illness he became increasingly withdrawn from life to the point of being almost totally detached from the world, to the point of complete indifference, grief, and insufferable sadness. Then one day, dramatically and strangely, he is aroused from his stupor. I continue in Myshkin's words:

"I was finally roused from this gloomy state, I remember, one evening on reaching Switzerland at Bale, and I was roused by the bray of an ass in the marketplace. I was immensely struck with the ass, and for some reason extraordinarily pleased with it, and suddenly everything seemed to clear up in my head. I've been awfully fond of asses ever since; they have a special attraction for me. I began to ask about them because I'd never seen one before, and I understood at once what a useful creature it was—industrious, strong, patient, cheap, long-suffering. And so, through the ass, all Switzerland began to attract me, so that my melancholy passed completely."

[Madame Epanchin remarks:]

"That's all very strange, but you can pass over the ass; let's come to something else. Why do you keep laughing. Aglaia? And you Adelaida? The prince told us splendidly about the ass. He has seen it himself, but what have you seen? You've never been abroad."

"I have seen an ass, maman," said Adelaida.

"And I've even heard one," asserted Aglaia (3, pp. 52-53).

This is a humorous incident from the vantage point of the Epanchins, but they all missed its particular and special relevance as a formative experience in Myshkin's recovery, as a significant event in the restoration of Myshkin to his own senses, and the re-emergence of his interest in the world and his wish to live.

I do not mean to imply that all people regard the honest man as a fool, or mistrust him or treat him as a puzzle. My point is that honesty can never be understood through explanation and analysis. Honesty exists only as itself, and must be recognized in its pure form. Efforts to explain, justify, or defend often lead to further alienation in relationships, and a sense of hopelessness and despair. Myshkin, at one point, frightened and agitated, on the verge of a breakdown, attempts to explain himself and to defend his being-in-the-world:

I want to explain everything, everything, everything! Oh, yes! You think I'm Utopian? A Theorist? My ideas are really all so simple. . . . Don't you believe it? You smile? You know I'm contemptible sometimes, for I lose my faith. As I came here just now, I wondered: "How shall I talk to him?

> With what words shall I begin, so that they may understand a little?" How frightened I was, but I was more frightened for you. It was awful, awful! And yet, how could I be afraid? Wasn't it shameful to be afraid? What does it matter that for one advanced man there is such a mass of retrograde and evil ones? That's what I'm so happy about; that I'm convinced now that there is no such mass, and that it's all living material! There's no reason to be troubled because we're absurd, is there? You know it really is true that we're absurd, that we're shallow, have bad habits, that we're bored, that we don't know how to look at things, that we can't understand; we're all like that, all of us, you, and I, and they! And you are not offended at my telling you to your faces that you're absurd? Are you? And if that's so, aren't you good material? Do you know, to my thinking it's a good thing sometimes to be absurd; it's better in fact, it makes it easier to forgive one another, it's easier to be humble (3, pp. 536-537).

The honest person is supported and valued at times, but almost inevitably his motives are questioned. He suffers in a world where the fool and the sucker are ravaged, in a world where all the strength and resources of the self are sometimes not enough to maintain a state of health. Myshkin's disintegration, daily reinforced by his awareness of human misery and cruelty, illustrates the inevitable defeat of a truly good and honest man in a morally bankrupt society; and is final proof of the inability of any man to bear the burden of moral perfection in an imperfect world.

The honest person wants to live his life his own way, to express himself directly, in a way consistent with his own experience. What idle nonsense it is to see hidden meanings and dynamics, unconscious motivations, thwarted impulses, in even simple expressions! The primary experiences of his senses exist as valid and significant in their own right and are the important resources in an authentic existence. Analyzing the simple, everyday truths of the eyes and ears and heart as complicated expressions of frustrated purposes and goals, as psychic conflicts, is all part of the peculiar game now being played for higher and higher stakes.

The honest man has conflicts but they are not buried in some dreaded past. The conflict is one of choice:

whether to be truthful though suffering and causing pain, or whether to maintain a false life in favor of economic and social gains. A person living according to his own nature often must choose between honesty and kindness. Even when honest words are stated gently and expressed quietly and directly, they may result in pain and suffering for others. Sometimes it is difficult to speak honestly when one knows that the other person is struggling to emerge, is already surrounded by criticism and rejection, and one knows that what one says will deeply hurt.

And yet I wonder at times whether my being kind and gentle is not a dodge, an escape from facing the other person, from facing the experience, from facing the issue. I wonder if in actuality the relationship is not weakened, when I act out of kindness though my inner desire or wish or experience pulls me in another direction. Do I choose to be kind in such moments because truth is more painful to bear, more uncertain in its effects, more apt to foment unrest and disturbance in a relationship? I have never fully accepted myself when I have been kind at the expense of being honest. As I think through the value involved, I realize that every dishonest act, even when it is motivated by sympathy and support, is a denial of the self. Yet there are times when I choose kindness over honesty, even when it causes anguish within me, because I cannot bring myself to hurt another human being—particularly when the person is already suffering and alone, already feeling belittled and friendless.

Still, I struggle with this issue, and each time I come up against it, I meet it fresh and new. Ideally, only by saying what I really believe and feel can I participate in reality in a fundamental and healthy sense. The significance of being honest was once brought home to me in a moving conflict involving a father, a mother, and their young son. To convey this confrontation, and a small boy's desire to keep his word, I quote a lengthy passage from a book published in 1906.

> Our courtyard is full of children and my little boy has picked a bosom friend out of the band: his name is Einar and he can be as good as another.
>
> My little boy admires him and Einar allows himself to

be admired, so that the friendship is established on the only proper basis. . . .

Now something big and unusual takes place in our courtyard and makes an extraordinary impression on the children and gives their small brains heaps to struggle with for many a long day.

The scarlatina comes.

And scarlatina is not like a pain in your stomach, when you have eaten too many pears, or like a cold, when you have forgotten to put on your jacket. Scarlatina is something quite different, something powerful and terrible. It comes at night and takes a little boy who was playing quite happily that same evening. And then the little boy is gone. . . .

Day by day, the little band is being thinned out and not one of them has yet come back.

I stand at my open window and look at my little boy, who is sitting on the steps below with his friend. They have their arms around each other's necks and see no one except each other; that is to say, Einar sees himself and my little boy sees Einar.

"If you fall ill, I will come and see you," says my little boy.

"No, you won't!"

"I will come and see you."

His eyes beam at this important promise. Einar cries as though he were already ill.

And the next day he is ill.

He lies in a little room all by himself. No one is allowed to go to him. A red curtain hangs before the window.

My little boy sits alone on the steps outside and stares up at the curtain. His hands are thrust deep into his pockets. He does not care to play and he speaks to nobody.

And I walk up and down the room, uneasy to what will come next.

"You are anxious about our little boy," says his mother. "And it will be a miracle if he escapes."

"It's not that. We've all had a touch of scarlatina."

But just as I want to talk to her about it, I hear a fumbling with the door-handle which there is no mistaking and then he stands before us in the room.

I know you so well, my little boy, when you come in sideways like that, with a long face, and go and sit in a corner and look at the two people who owe so much happiness to you—look from one to the other. Your eyes are greener than usual. You can't find your words and you sit huddled up and you are ever so good.

"Mother, is Einar ill?"

"Yes, but the doctor says that he is not so bad."

"Is he infectious, Mother?"

"Yes, he is. His little sister has been sent to the country, so that she may not fall ill too. No one is allowed to go to him except his mother, who gives him his milk and his medicine and makes his bed."

A silence.

The mother of my little boy looks down at her book and suspects nothing. The father of my little boy looks in great suspense from the window.

"Mother, I want to go to Einar."

"You can't go there, my little man. You hear, he's infectious. Just think, if you should fall ill yourself! Einar isn't bothering at all about chatting with you. He sleeps the whole day long."

"But when he wakes, Mother?"

"You can't go up there."

This tells upon him and he is nearly crying. I see that the time has come for me to come to his rescue:

"Have you promised Einar to go and see him?" I ask.

"Yes, Father. . . ."

He is over his trouble. His eyes beam. He stands erect and glad beside me and puts his little hand in mine.

"Then of course you must do so," I say, calmly. "So soon as he wakes."

Our mother closes her book with a bang:

"Go down to the courtyard and play, while Father and I have a talk."

The boy runs away.

And she comes up to me and lays her hand on my shoulder and says, earnestly:

"I daren't do that, do you hear?"

And I take her hand and kiss it and say, quite as earnestly:

"And I daren't *refuse!*"

We look at each other, we two, who share the empire, the power and the glory.

"I heard our little boy make his promise," I say, "I saw him. Sir Galahad himself was not more in earnest when swearing his knightly oath. You see; we have no choice here. He can catch the scarlatina in any case and it is not even certain that he will catch it. . . ."

"If it was diphtheria, you wouldn't talk like that!"

"You may be right. But am I to become a thief for the sake of a nickel, because I am not sure that I could resist the temptation to steal a kingdom?"

"You would not find a living being to agree with you."

"Except yourself. And that is all I want. The infection is really only a side matter. It can come this way or that way. We can't safeguard him, come what may. . . ."

"But are we to send him straight to where it is?"

"We're not doing that; it's not we who are doing that."

She is very much excited. I put my arm around her waist and we walk up and down the room together:

"Darling, today our little boy may meet with a great misfortune. He may receive a shock from which he will never recover. . . ."

"That is true," she says.

"If he doesn't keep his promise, the misfortune has occurred. It would already be a misfortune if he could ever think that it was possible for him to break it, if it appeared to him that there was anything great or remarkable about keeping it."

"Yes, but. . . ."

"Darling, the world is full of careful persons. One step more and they become mere paltry people. Shall we turn that into a likely thing, into a virtue, for our little boy? His promise was stupid: let that pass. . . ."

"He is so little."

"Yes, that he is; and God be praised for it! Think what good luck it is that he did not know the danger, when he made his promise, that he does not understand it now, when he is keeping it. What a lucky beggar! He is learning to keep his word, just as he has learnt to be clean. By the time that he is big enough to know his danger, it will be an indispensable habit with him. And he gains all that at the risk of a little scarlatina."

She lays her head on my shoulder and says nothing more.

That afternoon, she takes our little boy by the hand and goes up with him to Einar. They stand on the threshold of his room, bid him good-day and ask him how he is.

Einar is not at all well and does not look up and does not answer.

But that does not matter in the least (4).

In this family crisis we see the way in which differences are resolved and honesty is maintained. We see that through the open, direct confrontation between the mother and the father a deeper sense of family solidarity emerges.

Kindness at the expense of honesty creates false impressions and distorts experiences of reality, but it may temporarily soften the pain and lighten the burdens of life. Honesty at the expense of kindness creates suffering, horror, and impotency though it also provides the only basis for an authentic existence, for self-growth, individuality, and for genuine relations with others.

Often being honest means being different from what one has been before. Suddenly, a new characteristic, idea, or attitude emerges in another person, one that we view with disbelief. We expect consistency and when the person behaves differently we are surprised and sometimes shocked.

We are deeply shaken when those we love turn on us in angry tones or suddenly reproach us. Yet many of these situations involve a choice between honesty and kindness. In kindness, we continue to be as we are, meeting others with a consistency of feeling, being supportive and helpful. But the self is always developing in new directions. Sometimes the struggle leads to morbid moods that can create pain and otherwise disturb a relationship in vital ways. Yet if one maintains honesty, living through the misery it sometimes brings, deeper bonds are established and a new beauty and awareness emerge, in the end, which fill life with great joy.

The attitude of honesty in a relationship in psychotherapy is conveyed in an essay by Rebecca M. Osborne. With reference to the severely disturbed individual, she writes:

> He senses the shallowness of much of what passes as friendship and the envy and jealousy that lurks in the background of so many family relationships. All of these individuals become part of the conspiracy of *them*. Only the one who can come to the mental patient with genuine acceptance and forbearance in his eyes, saying by his manner as well as his words, "I do not see what you see, but I believe you when you say *you* see it. I believe that you do feel what you claim to feel. Let's talk it over:"—only such a one can win the deep confidence of the mentally ill person (6, pp. 26-28).

Whether to choose honesty or kindness in a conflict is not a matter of choosing which is better. Rather it is the decision of a particular self in a concrete moment of existence. Who can say for others whether being and growth are higher values than kindness and the happiness of a gentle laugh? Each person finds his own way in a moment of life, when theory is totally outside. Then the immediacy of two selves facing each other create the reality of a joyful experience or one of grief.

The question of honesty first arose in my mind as a serious problem in psychotherapy when I talked with a child about his terrible school existence and the child asked me for an opinion, "Do you believe Mr. Radcliffe should scream at us and hurt us with a ruler when we don't do what he tells us?" And another time when an old man inquired, "Tell me where I went wrong. What did I do to bring so much misery and unhappiness in our lives. Just give me some sign that the evil can be erased, that I can begin to find some decency, some basis for life." Then again with a weary mother whose "mentally-retarded" child had experienced one rejection after another in many schools, a mother who had searched long and exhaustively to find a place where her son could belong. Finally, in defeat, she exclaimed, "There isn't any place for him. No school wants him. No one is willing to help. Why is it that people in the neighborhood avoid and shun him? He is one of our own kind!" And the adolescent who spoke triumphantly and sadistically about the pleasure he derived from throwing a handicapped neighbor down the basement steps, splitting his forehead, and making necessary an emergency visit to the hospital —and seven stitches. This young man inquired of me, "Isn't it good for me to feel a victory at last? I've been stepped on and tricked all my life. Now I'm beginning to get even and settle the score. There's nothing wrong with that, is there?"

Each time I held my own feelings in check. Even when my whole being urged a position, urged expression, a part of me held back. I did not speak except to encourage the individual to explore further the nature of his own feeling, thinking, and experience. Only later did I realize that in many moments of life clarification and understanding are not enough. Reflections and commentary do not spread to the root of life where no man has lived before. Interpretations too often skirt the edge of existence, stay within the bounds of professional theory and practice, and fail to penetrate the all in one in a transcending dialogue—a dialogue of truth and conviction that alone can unite two persons in a genuine human bond.

Only after much internal dissension did I realize that in many instances *to understand* another person is to place him on a lower scale of life. It is a kind of leveling process in which a superior insight and intellect grasps its subject and sees into and beyond the surface words and feelings. Yet this seeing into and beyond another places the subject in a category. *He* is to be understood. *He* is to change so that I may know my efforts have not been in vain. So that I may measure my success.

I began at times to think, "I want to speak, to say what's in my heart and mind, to meet the other simply and directly, to come alive with my own expressed conviction." At the same time, I also believed that each person must find his own way by the light of his own perceptions, meanings, and values. But the struggle and the search continued until one day I wondered, "Isn't it rather God-like of you to think that your expressed feeling and conviction will influence another human being away from his own quantum in life? Aren't you assuming a power over others that in itself implies a view of others as being so fragile and malleable that external ideas will quickly transform them? And doesn't this distort your own experience with individuals, even those who are faced with deep and penetrating conflicts and problems, who in spite of all their suffering have resisted ideas and beliefs that challenged and denied their own perceptions and experiences?"

The struggle went on until I realized that an issue could not be settled in advance by theory or assumption or concept or method but only by life.

Honesty is not an old-fashioned virtue, an ideal that has no place in modern life but rather it is a vital requirement of growth in self and this requirement perhaps is not completely and purely realized in everyday life, but still it remains unyieldingly present in the self. Only as one speaks honestly is there real hope for continued self identity, and for fundamental meeting. As long as one departs from the truth, one continues to remain a stranger to himself and to others.

The lie, that distortion of reality, is one of the most pervasive evils of our time. Whether honesty is denied for self-protection or for self-aggrandizement, its denial is inevitably a form of manipulation—and manipulation is responsible for much of the human misery, grief and suffering in the world. I believe that every action, overt or implicit, motivated by a desire to change other persons is a form of manipulation. Although the wish to change others is sometimes couched in altruistic terms, and sometimes even exists as a pure wish for the health and welfare of the other, it still remains as a desire to change and as a form of manipulation if only by remote control. B. F. Skinner puts it this way: "If, in working with a patient or student or friend, one arranges conditions so that he becomes more active than before and more adaptive, this is progress, but it is also control" (8, p. 576). I agree that control and manipulation are present if one *arranges* conditions *in order* to change others. But, if progress occurs, not through arrangement of conditions, not through predetermined goals and criteria for evaluation, but through genuine spontaneous encounters, then growth occurs naturally as people live together openly and honestly. The honest person is concerned solely in being as he is, in letting himself grow in life through inquiry, through expressive forms, in his relations with others. If being one's self has meaning and value for others, if in itself it opens channels of sensitivity, awareness, and discovery in others, then it is like all living substances that awaken in us new dimensions of thought and feeling.

I am attempting here to make a distinction between making resources available that may be chosen or not; and the calculated use of particular methods and materials in order to change thoughts, feelings and behavior. In a sense, the shrewd, clever, facile, sleight-of-hand expert is in command over others but, inwardly, such a person suffers. To deceive and manipulate, to trick with clever tactics is a basic illness of modern society that severs the individual self from its own moorings and eventually destroys any sense of unique identity and authentic existence. The tragedy is that we take others with us in the deterioration of our self-respect and human integrity.

When we are not honest, part of us is buried and a new, false, distorted image replaces the real self. A significant stream of life is removed—a stream that emerged in the first place to meet life, to know persons in the fullest sense, to realize opportunities, to face and resolve the challenges, issues, and problems of existence.

I have come to believe that every form of dishonesty is immoral and is a powerful deterrent to authentic growth and to the development of the real self. No matter how much I try to deceive myself that by remaining silent I am being non-committal, when my silence is a form of deception I let the truth remain hidden. No matter how much I feel I am following a *professional* ethic when I dodge a question, there are times when I know inwardly a *human* ethic is being violated and I am engaging, through manipulation, in dishonest behavior. No matter how I convince myself that kindness assuages the suffering of others, when it is given at the expense of honesty I know that it is tenuous and false. No matter how much I reassure myself that my desire to change another person is for his own good, I know that this wish to change others, even though it leads to "improvement," is an act of manipulation and therefore a form of dishonesty. If I tell a person that my interest is in changing his personality, he may resent it. But even if he does not, it still violates my own belief in autonomy, in the private destiny of each man, and in the responsibility of each self to find its own values in life. Even when the other person sees my desire to change him as a virtue, it still remains as the imposition of the views and ideals of one self onto another.

When an individual hides behind a screen of objectivity there is always a danger that he will evade individual responsibility and successfully control others by remaining anonymous. Such a protective device makes a true meeting between persons impossible and is a mask which contributes to the alienation which characterizes man in our time.

Is man so entrapped in ambition, distortion, and turmoil that he is simply unable to experience the wonder and beauty of life? Is it impossible for man today to relate to sources in the universe that give rise to tenderness and joy? What is it in man or in society that makes it necessary to complicate and obfuscate the simple truths and values in life? How is it that man can see the radiant colors of the rainbow and the beautiful sunburst at dawn and not experience grandeur and ecstasy? How can man fail to discover authentic beauty in all that surrounds him?

There is so much in the world to pull and tug at me, to arouse within me a sense of optimism, to bring me back to life in all its promise. Then I see the universe as a new creation: The moment of quiet, the silence of rustling leaves, the feel of my footsteps on gathering pine needles, the gentle wind blowing against my face, the soft mist which shrouds the world in a mysterious beauty, the loving message in twinkling eyes, the resonant quality in a compassionate human voice.

Everywhere, all around, we are in the midst of genuine life, yet we reach out and strive for confused and entangled goals, as if the distant star held more meaning and challenge than the immediate and simple truth.

## REFERENCES

1. BUBER, MARTIN. *Between Man and Man.* London: Routledge and Kegan Paul Ltd., 1947.
2. BUBER, MARTIN. *Hasidism and Modern Man.* New York: Horizon Press, Inc., 1958.
3. DOSTOEVSKI, FYODOR. *The Idiot.* New York: Bantam Books, Inc., 1958.
4. EWALD, CARL. *My Little Boy.* New York: Charles Scribner's Sons, 1906.
5. LEE, DOROTHY. *Freedom and Culture.* Englewood Cliffs, New Jersey: Prentice-Hall, Inc., 1955.
6. OSBORNE, REBECCA M. The Mental Patient and the Sense of Conspiracy. *Inward Light,* Vol. 33, Fall, 1960.
7. SHLIEN, JOHN. The Client-centered Approach to Schizophrenia: A First Approximation. *Psychotherapy of the Psychoses.* Ed. by Arthur Burton. New York: Basic Books, 1960.
8. SKINNER, B. F. Cultural Evolution as Viewed by Psychologists. *Daedalus,* Vol. 90, Summer, 1961.

# 6

# Beyond Good and Evil

Since the dawn of Western civilization attempts have been made to formulate a code of ethics to safeguard man's humanity to man. Statutes throughout history have attempted to control human behavior and to point to right and wrong, to justice and injustice in human affairs. While rulers were evolving laws governing good and evil, religious prophets were propounding the doctrine that the good man will receive his just reward and the evil man will suffer hell and damnation. The Ten Commandments, Adam's fall from virtue, and the tales of Satan, are but a few of the dramatic illustrations of religious formulations of good and evil.

Society has constructed and elaborated notions of right and wrong in human affairs, and has dictated appropriate contacts among people to protect the individual and tc safeguard the welfare of the state. Conformity to these social rules is inculcated, both directly and indirectly, at an early age: the conforming, obedient child is taught he is good, while the unruly, deviant child learns he is naughty. Social, religious, and legal precepts define good and evil and impose these standards on the individual through group pressures and the institutions of society. Good, thus created, emerges not as a value in its own right, not as a quality intrinsic to being human, but out of a fear of the consequences of being bad. Good exists as a reaction to evil, as a fixed set of laws and standards that protect society from the "evil" individual and protect man from himself. As Nietzsche puts it (10, p. 112):

> . . . this morality defends itself with its might; stubbornly and inexorably it says, I myself am morality itself and nothing other than myself is morality! With the aid of a religion, in fact, which agreed with and flattered the most sublime desires of herd-animals, we have come to the point where

even in the political and social institutions an increasingly visible expression of this morality can be found.

Thus, the conformist is good and the rebel is evil for almost everything that lifts the individual above the herd produces fear in his neighbor and is called evil (10).

The man who does not sin, who does not transgress the laws which safeguard society and his fellow man, is a good man. He chooses good over evil, not as an affirmative expression of a real value, but as an act of self-protection and self-preservation. To be good out of fear of the consequences of evil, out of fear of imprisonment or social rejection or eternal damnation, means to choose the system, regardless of one's own self and one's own experience. The system or social rule guides and determines the articles of faith and beliefs by which men live—not what man experiences as good but what is ordained as such religiously, socially, legally.

Moral philosophers have not been satisfied with conceptions of good and evil that are rooted in self-protection and self-preservation. They have explored the essence of the good as a quality positively present and connected to healthy, creative life in the individual self. They have been concerned with the personal and human value of the good.

Philosophers have described kinds of goodness and qualities of goodness. They have employed analogous terms, such as God, love, truth, beauty, justice, harmony, unity, order. But they have not come to grips with an absolute concept of goodness itself or the ultimate meaning of evil. For example, Plato in *The Republic* equates God and good, and presents good, not as the opposite of evil, but as in a totally different realm. The dialogue between Socrates and Adeimantus (12, p. 75) proceeds as follows:

> God is always to be represented as he truly is . . .
> Right.
> And is he not truly good? And must he not be represented as such?
> Certainly.
> And no good thing is hurtful?
> No indeed.

And that which is not hurtful hurts not?

Certainly not.

And that which hurts not does no evil?

No.

And can that which does no evil be a cause of evil?

Impossible.

And the good is advantageous?

Yes.

And therefore the cause of well-being?

Yes.

It follows therefore that the good is not the cause of all things, but of the good only?

Assuredly.

Then God, if he be good, is not the author of all things, as the many assert, but he is the cause of a few things only, and not of most things that occur to men. For few are the goods of human life, and many are the evils, and the good is to be attributed to God alone; of the evils the causes are to be sought elsewhere, and not in him.

Yet Plato is not always consistent. In *Phaedo* (11, p. 91) Socrates explains that everything that admits of generation is generated from opposites and in no other way. Thus the stronger comes from the weaker, beauty from ugliness, right from wrong, big from little. Following this logic, good must come from evil. Plato says that anything that has a saving and improving element is good; the corrupting and destroying element is evil. Mildew is the evil of corn, rot of timber, rust of copper. That which is a true part of one's own nature is good; the evil is that which is foreign, contrived, accidental. In everything there is an inherent good and an inherent evil.

Plato reveals and describes the four virtues, the four qualities of goodness: courage, temperance, wisdom, and justice; and the characteristics of evil: injustice, intemperance, cowardice, and ignorance. But he does not tell what good is; he only describes its attributes.

Aristotle in his books on ethics also describes the qualities of goodness. He explains that the good may be viewed in three different ways: as good in itself, in some quality it has, or in some relation it bears to something else (2, p. 32). But the essence of goodness, what it is in itself, is by its very nature prior to any of its qualities or its relation to something else. For Aristotle there are degrees of goodness, with happiness having the highest degree of finality, the highest degree of self-sufficiency. We choose happiness for its own sake and that alone; whereas honor, pleasure, wisdom, and other qualities, though good in themselves, are nevertheless chosen because they contribute to our happiness.

For Epictetus (5, pp. 103-104) the essence of God is expressed in the essence of the human being. And the essence of the human being is knowledge, intellect, reason, because these attributes distinguish him from plants and animals. In these he attains uniqueness. The opposite of these qualities, ignorance and irrationality, constitutes evil.

St. Augustine (13) holds a different view of good and evil. He makes good and being the same. He says: "So long therefore as they are, they are good; therefore whatsoever is, is good." The evil is that which is false, that which is unharmonized and in a state of disorder, that which does not fit or belong. St. Thomas Aquinas (1) takes a similar position: being, the true, the one, and the good are by their very nature one in reality.

Hume (8), on the other hand, sees the good as that which contributes to the peace and security of man in society; morality is that which promotes the welfare of society. For Hegel (7) the good is a universal which requires individuality to give it life and movement; gifts, capacities and powers constitute spiritual life and these are realized only in individuality. The good is implicitly inherent in real truth; it is simply *being* itself.

From this brief philosophical inquiry we can see that different attributes have been selected as virtues: temperance, justice, wisdom, courage, happiness, intelligence, being, harmony, order, reason, knowledge, peace, and security of society. The indicators of evil are: intemperance, injustice, foolishness, misery, ignorance, irrationalism, disharmony, disorder, war, disturbance. Each of these definitions describes good or evil in terms of primary characteristics but none of them answers the question: What is goodness in general (6)? G. E. Moore (9, pp. 6-9) justifies this failure as follows:

> If I am asked "What is good?" my answer is that good is good, and that is the end of the matter. Or if I am asked, "How is good defined?" my answer is that it cannot be defined, and that is all I have to say about it. But disappointing as these answers may appear, they are of the very last importance . . . My point is that "good" is a simple notion, just as "yellow" is a simple notion; that, just as you cannot, by any manner of means, explain to anyone who does not already know it, what yellow is, so you cannot explain what good is . . . The most important sense of "definition" is that in which a definition states what are the parts which invariably compose a certain whole; and in this sense "good" has no definition because it is simple and has no parts.

Robert S. Hartman (6) in a recent essay, commenting on the failure of philosophers to provide a definition of goodness in itself, defines the good as that which has all the properties it is supposed to have. For example, a man is good if he is conscious of himself, if he has all the qualities he is supposed to have. The properties of a man attain virtue because a particular man defines them as dimensions of his own being.

Martin Buber offers a similar definition (4). For him, the man who is true to himself is a good man; the man who is false to himself is evil. Man has but one choice, the path of rightness or the path of evil, the path of being or the path of non-being. To be good is to be real, authentic, true; to be bad is to be fictitious, false, unauthentic. Truth is an expression of goodness; the lie is an act of evil. Good and evil are alternative paths; the individual alone, in his own being, or failure to be, chooses between them. For Buber, good and evil are not opposites or extremes of the same reality but rather they are fundamentally dissimilar in nature, structure, and dynamics. The concrete good or the concrete evil can be known as specific events in a man's life during moments of contemplation and self-absorption.

Only the individual himself can determine the rightness or wrongness of his action. This, he must determine on the basis of whether or not it is an actualization of a real self or a false, externalized representation. Evil concerns itself with possibilities; good is always an immediate and immanent reality. Even at his peak, the evil person merely replaces an *undirected possibility* with an *undirected reality* in which he does that which is alien to himself. The good is always directed. The good person chooses the one stretched beam; the one taut string. For the good, there is only one direction, one true path; for the evil person there are many alternatives, many possibilities. The good is a decisive act of the whole self; evil is fraught with indecision and possibility growing out of a detached and fragmented self. Evil needs no confirmation; it reinforces itself as the safe, secure, and wise course. In contrast, the good person requires confirmation, which includes a self-knowledge that is congruent with action. Buber puts it this way (4, p. 136):

> Man as man is an audacity of life, undetermined and unfixed; he therefore requires confirmation, and he can naturally only receive this as an individual man, in that others and he himself confirm him in his being-this-man. Again and again the Yes must be spoken to him, from the look of the confidant and from the stirrings of his own heart, to liberate him from the dread of abandonment, which is a fore-taste of death. At a pinch, one can do without confirmation from others if one's own reaches such a pitch that it no longer needs to be supplemented by the confirmation of others. But not vice-versa: the encouragement of his fellow-men does not suffice if self-knowledge demands inner rejection, for self-knowledge is incontestably the more reliable.

The ultimate good is the choosing of oneself, even when one's being is not confirmed by others and is independent of all findings. Buber is emphatic on this point (4, p. 138):

> . . . he must bring the principle of his own self-affirmation, nothing else must remain worthy of affirmation than just that which is affirmed by him; his Yes to himself determines the reason and right of affirmation. If he still concedes any significance to the concept "good" it is this: precisely that which I am.

Hartman defines the good in similar terms. He says (6, p. 13):

> Thus what I have to do to fulfill my definition (of the good) is to *define* myself, to answer the question: "Who am I? And Who am I?" I am I. This is my defense of myself—

pure self-awareness: I am I. The concept I have to fulfill is "I", or "I am I" and when I fulfill this I am a good "I."

The recognition of the self as the supreme value and the identification of goodness with authenticity, with precisely that "which I am," does not mean that man is inherently good. What man *is* at any particular moment of his life may be good, but man as such is neither good nor evil. Man is born neither with grace nor in sin. In any moment of his life he has a choice. Man may choose to be, and when he does he participates in goodness; but man may also choose not to be, that is, he may choose to be evil rather than good.

The actualization of man's capacities and talents toward increasing individuation and uniqueness, toward a particular, incomparable selfhood is an index of the nature of man. But being human also means living in a world of safety, of possibility, of isolation, of embeddedness. Self-preservation cannot be regarded as evil except by external viewing and labeling, for it is as much a human reality as the sudden, spontaneous, esthetic creation. It is within the nature of man to protect and maintain that which is known to provide safety and satisfaction. Man, in his history, has often chosen the safe rather than the courageous. But also he has often chosen death and destruction over life and creation.

If good is desirable and evil is undesirable; if good is a virtue and evil a sin, then the fault lies with human construction itself for every man in many moments of his life is "evil" and every man is "good." Much evil has derived from "good," and much that is good has resulted from so-called evil. Furthermore, all good is evil in the sense that it blocks a greater good from emerging. That which has been defined as good can become stagnant, static, and embedded. That which is known as good can become evil and that which is evil can become good.

Evil is good in that it motivates good. Without evil, good could not exist. Good becomes meaningful in contrast to evil; it attains reality by the presence of evil. Together good and evil exist as dimensions of man's unity and wholeness. George Berkeley (3, p. 144) puts it this way:

> As for the mixture of pain or uneasiness which is in the world, pursuant to the general Laws of Nature, and the actions of finite, imperfect spirits, this, in the state we are in at present, is indispensably necessary to our well-being. But our prospects are too narrow. We take, for instance, the idea of some one particular pain into our thoughts, and account it evil; whereas, if we enlarge our view, so as to comprehend the various ends, connexions, and dependencies of things, on what occasions and in what proportions we are affected with pain and pleasure, the nature of human freedom, and the design with which we are put into the world; we shall be forced to acknowledge that those particular things, which, considered in themselves, appear to be evil, have the nature of good, when considered as linked with the whole system of beings.

Perhaps what we must recognize today is not the good and the evil in human behavior but the fact that man is pressed from all sides to conform. In the light of these constant pressures for conformity, man needs to be encouraged to be himself. A strong and vital stand needs to be taken in behalf of creative selfhood, not because it is all there is to man or because it is all good in contrast to the evil of conformity, but because real individuality is so widely repressed and denied. Left to himself, man will find his own quantum in life; he will choose to be or not to be in the light of the resources and conditions and challenges that he meets.

Unfortunately, man today is largely prevented from making a free choice. Doubt and suspicion surround the individual. He is pressed to move in particular directions. He deliberately goes contrary to his own self-knowledge. He fails to protest when this would enable him to grow. He does protest as a reaction to the external when order and system would integrate him and bring balance and harmony to his life. He chooses not to be when the inner voice calls for an expression of being and self-affirmation. He chooses assertive being when quiet withdrawal and solitude are appropriately human. Because modern man is so surrounded and pressed to strive for standards and values and goals that contradict his own growing humanity, he must actively confirm his selfhood to prevent his becoming a thing, a commodity, a machine.

The existential and humanist concerns with good and evil are aimed at promoting man's creative emergence as an individual self, not as a mere life but a life with meaning, life with zest, life with self-structure and self-expansion.

Today official society directs its power and influence toward security, self-preservation, and consequently toward conformity and the socialization of the individual. Fear is used to promote freedom from fear. In his book, *Beyond Good and Evil,* Nietzsche expresses this point of view most effectively (10, p. 137):

> Today, when in Europe the herd-animal alone is honored and alone doles out the honors, when "Equality of rights" could all too easily turn into equality of wrong-doings—by which I mean the joint war on everything rare, strange, privileged; on superior men, superior souls, superior duties, superior responsibilities, on creative fullness of powers and the ability to rule—today the concept of greatness must embrace the spirit who is distinguished, who wants to be himself, who can be different, who can stand alone, and who must live by his own resources. A philosopher reveals something of his own ideal when he legislates that "The greatest shall be the one most capable of solitude, the most hidden, the most deviative, the man beyond good and evil, the master of his virtues, the one whose will can overflow. *Greatness* shall consist in being as many-faceted as one is whole, as wide as one is full.

The counter influence of the humanist position is necessary to nourish and encourage the expression of true being, the importance of man's being himself. Non-being, that is, conformity to external standards and values, is not the more powerful impulse in man; but it is more strongly encouraged by modern society, and it easily squelches being because it advances materialism and expansive technology. A counter revolution is needed to promote the authentic capacities of particular, concrete individuals toward creative selfhood.

Humanism is not good in contrast to the evil of materialism. Both are aspects of man, reflecting and representing man's search for security and for creation and individuality. Both are dimensions of being human that have been expressed throughout history as man has struggled to maintain his identity while evolving in the world.

## REFERENCES

1. AQUINAS, ST. THOMAS. *Truth.* Chicago: Henry Regnery Co., 1952.
2. ARISTOTLE. *The Ethics of Aristotle.* Tr. by James A. K. Thomason. Baltimore: Penguin Books, Inc., 1955.
3. BERKELEY, GEORGE. *The Principles of Human Knowledge.* Ed. by G. J. Warnock. New York: World Publishing Co., 1963.
4. BUBER, MARTIN. *Good and Evil.* New York: Charles Scribner's Sons, 1952.
5. EPICTETUS. *Discourses and Enchiridion.* Tr. by Thomas W. Higginson. New York: Walter J. Black, 1944.
6. HARTMAN, ROBERT S. *Individual in Management.* Unpublished paper. Nationwide Management Center, Columbus, Ohio, 1963.
7. HEGEL, G. W. F. *The Phenomenology of the Mind.* Tr. by J. B. Baillie, New York: The Macmillan Co., 1931.
8. HUME, DAVID. *An Inquiry Concerning Human Understanding.* New York: The Bobbs-Merrill Co., Inc., 1955.
9. MOORE, GEORGE E. *Principia Ethica.* Cambridge: Cambridge University Press, 1903.
10. NIETZSCHE, FRIEDRICH. *Beyond Good and Evil.* Tr. by Marianne Cowan. Chicago: Henry Regnery Co., 1955.
11. PLATO. *The Last Days of Socrates.* Tr. by Hugh Tredenick. Baltimore: Penguin Books, Inc., 1954.
12. PLATO. *The Republic.* Tr. by B. Jowett. New York: Vintage Books, 1961.
13. ST. AUGUSTINE. *The Confessions of St. Augustine.* Chicago: Henry Regnery Co., for Great Books Foundation.

7

# Ethical and Moral Value

Ethical and moral value (in the sense of this essay) has an integrative meaning which includes the ethical realm where intrinsic conscience points to rightness; the moral realm where there is a deep sense of love, justice, wisdom, beauty, and courage; and the realm of value where the ultimate worth of the unique and the universal in the individual and in mankind takes root and serves as a source of creation.

Truth, self-knowledge, and insight, without reference to ethic, are insufficient as values in man's search for meaning. Truth without character, without conscience, without human concern, fails to attain the heights of moral unity, the height of man's ideals. In the absence of an ethical focus, truth can be as destructive to man as it is enlightening.

Truth refers to actual existence but existence may stand out in a moral vacuum, as a sense of nothingness. To have value truth must include the moral realm, the virtue of being as well as being itself. It must incorporate substance in the spiritual sense. It must be present as an integrated organic reality and not simply as an intellectual characteristic. The essence in existence is as important a factor in any human situation as the genuineness and reality of existence itself.

Thomas Aquinas (1) says that in reality being, the true, the one, and the good are by their very nature one and the same. Maslow (12, p. 120) concluded, from his studies of the higher ideals and values in man, that no ideal could be defined in such a way so as to contradict or exclude any other value. In its ultimate or final sense, Maslow states, truth is beautiful, truth is good, truth is perfect, truth is just, truth is unitary.

Though I can understand viewing truth in these ways,

I find that such views do not always correspond to experience—that is, truth sometimes exists without ethic, without moral, without value. For example, the existence of leukemia is a matter of truth but it is not beautiful or just or good. That which is true—that is, real, genuine, correct, and lawful—may also be damaging, harmful, or impoverishing. The unique is not necessarily just or good. The real is not necessarily simple or perfect or whole. The correct or lawful is not necessarily just or beautiful or complete. The true may be without ethic or moral, and, consequently corrosive and ugly. Value is required to create a truth which is good, just, and beautiful, a truth with meaning and substance.

Being free to be means having freedom within an ethical and value sense. Freedom is necessary to maintain one's humanity; the denial of freedom is equivalent to giving up a human characteristic. Freedom, however, without value, can lead to destruction and chaos. Freedom within the framework of ethical and moral value means not only the will to choose (not simply capricious, unfettered choice, though this might be highly appropriate in a particular situation) but choice growing out of a knowledge of the good and a willingness to choose the good.

The spiritual, esthetic sense is intrinsically present in the ultimate sources of being. To be one's self in the deepest regions means to be rooted in the good, the just, the true. In Hartman's terms, a man is good if he has all the properties he is supposed to have, not only intellect, talent, freedom, choice, responsibility, but ethical and moral value. When these qualities or virtues are integrated or harmonized in a unified way the result is goodness. Thus Hartman (7, p. 13) defines the good man as follows:

> I am the one I am. And this is precisely the property I have to fulfill . . . I am I. Now strangely enough, I found in the Bible, when Moses asked God what is your name, God answered, I am I—I am the one I am, Jehovah. The definition showed me that I am made in the image of God.

When *to be* becomes *I am* in actualizing properties and virtues, then good is present—not only freedom and genuineness but also moral and ethical commitment and responsibility. This is what Aristotle (2, p. 35) calls the supreme good, the end that has the highest degree of finality. When men choose what is good for themselves this should coincide with the absolutely good. In our relations with others we sometimes go beyond the intellectual level to the emotional level but we do not often reach to the final end of goodness that involves the expression of ethical and moral value. The moment that the good is recognized as an object of being, it no longer exists for then the "I am" drifts into an object of being, and ceases to be the unitive force between the doing and the being itself. The "I" becomes only a fragment, for, there is always one more "I" that cannot be known because of its limitless and boundless nature (7, p. 27).

When I use the term good or right, I do not mean a property or thing that might be labeled as good. Rather I mean the ultimate moral sense, which is not a law or a definition but the law beyond the law, the internal directive that establishes meaning and value. Morality refers to *value*, not values but the one guiding, determining, necessary light that is ideal, lofty, universal—ideal in Bonner's sense (3) as that which gives meaning to reality while enabling that which *is* to become consistent, just, whole.

There is a vital relationship between moral value and human behavior, between one's philosophy and one's activities, between one's sense of rightness and goodness and one's perceptions, feelings, and thoughts. This relationship has not been fully recognized and understood. Too often the exclusive concern has been with behavior and with personal and social change that results in more effective living. Yet, in one sense, the moral realm is always present and influences the development of individual creativeness and the nature of interpersonal relations. Healthy individual and communal life require moral and ethical roots.

This does not mean that we should strive to construct final truths which will provide a system of values to be automatically applied in every situation. On the contrary, interaction which unites morality and truth is always expressed in a new and vital way, and sometimes involves a struggle for genuine meaning. In such a struggle, value should emerge as that which is good for man, both as an individual and as a species. Such an absolute value, however, can never have meaning as a rule or precept, but only in the existential engagement, in the struggle between persons or with life. Value which emerges in authentic existence is as old as human history and yet it is entirely new and fresh.

By value I do not mean a value system. Value is the absence of any system. It is an ultimate, final, absolute moral and ethic, which enhances goodness, touching the individual to the roots of his existence and contributing to universal goodness. Although self-choice, freedom of expression, and respect for the individual are important values in the evolution of a healthy personality, they do not permeate character unless they exist in a framework of morality and ethic, or as Kluckhohn (9) says, unless they can be justified morally and esthetically.

Value does not refer to preferences. Preferences are values but value is not a preference, an alternative among alternatives. Value refers to worth as an ingredient of being but also to an ingrained human condition that is infinite and enduring. The meaning of value I am attempting to convey is similar to Plato's discussion of love in *Symposium*. In Plato's words (16), it is:

> . . . unproduced, indestructible; neither subject to increase or decay; not partly beautiful and partly deformed; not at one time beautiful and at another time not; not beautiful in relation to one thing and deformed in relation to another; not here beautiful and there deformed; not beautiful in the estimation of one person and deformed in that of another; nor can this supreme beauty be figured to the imagination like a beautiful face, or beautiful hands, or any portion of the body, nor like any discourse, nor any science. Nor does it subsist in any other that lives or is, either in earth or in heaven, or in any other place; but it is eternally uniform and consistent, and monoeidic with itself. All other things are beautiful through a participation of it, with this condition, that although they are subject to production and decay, it never becomes more or less, or endures any change.

A value system refers to beliefs, expectations, and preferences, which offer direction and influence choice. But value is an integrating or unifying dimension of the self. It is the quality that renders the person whole in the concrete moments of encounter. As Dorothy Lee (10, p. 165) observes, we can speak about human value, but we cannot know it directly. We infer value through its expression in behavior. Suzuki (18, p. 95) says ". . . when all the values are shut up in the depths of the unconscious in the limbo of oblivion, we have the value in their genuine form." When we consider value, our inner experience is a feeling of something definite, something absolute, something essential to our life.

The moral or ethical premise is not an object or thing or concept that can be described. Value is arbitrary and stands by itself (11, p. 42). It is the simplest level of moral reality and, as such, is undefinable. G. E. Moore explains this position in the following passage (14, p. 7):

> Definitions of the kind that I was asking for, definitions which describe the real nature of the object or notion denoted by a word, and which do not merely tell us what the word is used to mean, are only possible when the object or notion in question is something complex. You can give a definition of a horse, because a horse has many different properties and qualities, all of which you can enumerate. But when you have enumerated them all, when you have reduced a horse to his simplest terms, then you can no longer define those terms. They are simply something which you think of or perceive, and to any one who cannot think of or perceive them, you can never, by definition, make their nature known.

Value involves a sense of rightness that is in the nature of a command or directive, but its origin or nature (apart from an intuitive awareness) remains a mystery. The inner directive (the sense of value) is a commitment to life and to the continuity and enhancement of life in its highest, most ideal forms. The really good is just so, no more, no less. The good is just-so-ness (18, p. 95). This just-so-ness is a unity and wholeness, a harmony of all dimensions of man.

In modern society, ethical and moral value is not a central force in the development of the individual. In education, the primary focus is on knowledge, skill, and professional competence. In psychotherapy, the concern is with change toward self-confidence, self-acceptance, realness in expression, openness to experience, increasing individuality. Family involvement is centered in socialization, enculturation, and adjustment.

But a man may be unusually competent and skillful as a murderer or thief. And a man filled with self-esteem and confidence may enjoy success, competition, and victory over others. A free and assertive personality may flourish, joyfully and reassuringly, in his manipulation of others as a way to physical and social benefits and satisfactions for himself. Muscular strength, for example, can be used for battering, defeating, crushing; or it can be a form of self-discipline. Knowledge can be used for belittling, terrorizing, aggrandizing, promoting class and caste prejudices; or it can be used in the direction of self-awareness and enlightenment, toward justice, truth, and wisdom. Independence and autonomy can be expressions of competition, exploitation, manipulation, power, authority; or such qualities can grow out of a desire to stand out as a real person, to be as one is, to evolve one's unique talents.

It is not enough that the teacher inculcate a thirst for learning, originality, and independence of thought. It is not enough that the therapist enable the development of autonomy, self-direction, spontaneity, and trust. It is not enough that the parent promote health, and personal and social effectiveness. It is not enough for society to condition the individual to a life of comfort, security, group adaptation, and adjustment. It is necessary, as Maslow claims, that education and therapy reach into the moral realm and achieve goodness by helping the individual to become more honest, good, just, beautiful, whole, integrated (13, p. 59).

Morality is relevant to healthy existence. Without the ethical and value dimension such gains in personality as release of tension, freedom in self-disclosure, and self-insight are destitute of enduring value. Moral geniuses are not required—but men are needed who are morally alive and able to communicate themselves directly with their fellow beings (4, p. 105).

Increasingly I have become aware that in institutions such as the church, the family, the school, the clinic, and society in general, we are not concerned in a living concrete sense with value, with moral, with ethic, or with the development of character. Yet it is the moral or ethical sense of such value which determines the use of freedom, knowledge, autonomy. In his studies of pure and practical reason, Kant found support for the existence of an absolute being which gives rise to a moral world. He (8, p. 472) concluded that:

> . . . there really exist pure moral laws which entirely *a priori* (without regard to empirical motives) determine the use of the freedom of any rational being, both with regard to what has to be done and what has not to be done, and that these laws are imperative absolutely (not hypothetically only on the supposition of other empirical ends) and therefore in every respect necessary.

The moral imperative is not the arbitrary ordinance of a transcendent tyrant; nor is it determined by utilitarian calculations or group conventions. The moral law is man's own essential nature appearing as commanding authority (19, p. 195).

A commitment to ethic, to moral, to value, comes in the form of a command, a command that exists as a resource, as a direction to the individual, and in man's relationship to man. Such a command derives meaning in present experience although it also reflects man's ethical tradition and history.

Meaning and value are not contained in a quality of mind or attitude. It is the meaning that must be recognized and understood, not the characteristic alone but the ethical and moral frame in which a human quality derives significance. Marianne Eckardt (6, p. 9) warns us, "While the phrase 'to know thyself' has been given much meaning by poets and philosophers, nevertheless, it still leaves us with the clinical experience that self-knowledge is not necessarily identical with more effective or contented living."

The discrepancy that may exist between healthy personality and healthy character was revealed clearly to me when I began to study in detail my experience, and that of other persons, in psychotherapy. I saw an individual could change from a frightened, withdrawn, guilt-ridden, dependent, repressed person to an open, assertive, real, independent, autonomous being without evolving in any way in a moral sense.

I remember Don, an adolescent, who changed from an inhibited, restricted individual to an outgoing, socially effective, open person. His parents and teachers regarded the change as a blessing. I, however, became somewhat alarmed when he began to boast about his victorious, competitive achievements over the peers to whom he had formerly felt distinctly inferior.

I was troubled further when he told me triumphantly how his mother would buy a new car with the money she would get from an auto insurance company. By prolonging the recovery of a foot injury, she would receive an increased settlement. Don thought his mother clever and reported excitedly how she had studied the judgments of previous cases and had obtained advice from lawyer friends. The goal was to "beat the insurance company at its own game"; strategy, watchful waiting, and feigned indifference on settlement were the key methods. When you had knowledge and influence on your side, you could badger, stall, exploit, get as much return or benefit as the situation would bring. I asked Don whether this was honest, whether it was a healthy solution. I questioned him about the meaning of justice in settling the claim, whether fairness and moderation were not more consistent with integrity and rightness. He laughed and said only a fool would fail to exploit the benefits to the limits; this was the typical and "normal" way of dealing with insurance companies on accident claims.

At times, our discussions were extremely heated, with Don expressing anger and disgust at what he considered stupid, naive, and unsophisticated expressions on my part. I asked whether virtue, honesty, truth, and justice were not important in life. Shortly after these confrontations (which unfortunately did not go deep enough or far enough or reach a point of healthy resolution), Don's mother terminated the therapy, saying that there was no longer a need for it since Don was now a happy person, achieving in school and successful in his contacts with others. But there was no evolution or development in character, in ethic, in value as I have discussed it here.

The ethical or moral realm is never fully ignored or obliterated in human situations. In education and in therapy (even when teachers and therapists wish to remain dedicated to a theory or to objective procedures), moral and ethical convictions are expressed, if only subtly and indirectly. Georgene Seward (17, p. 145) has pointed out that therapists' values are so deeply involved in the process of therapy that they are more than likely to determine the pattern of reconstruction regardless of "honorable intentions" to the contrary.

Any person concerned with change in others automatically implies that some or much about the other person is "inferior" or "bad" (4, p. 10). Value permeates our development and personality to such a degree that it can never entirely be left out of the picture (4). But it is not a central concern of everyday living.

Of course I am not suggesting that the educator, psychotherapist, or parent teach value—but only that the ethical or moral conviction be as much a center of attention in education as the achievement of knowledge and skill; as much the focus in therapy as the goals of freedom, self-expression, awareness, choice, and congruence; as much the focus in family life as developmental training and socialization.

Direct attempts to teach moral and ethical principles (in contrast to the emergence of value as a dimension of being) are apt to result in failure or in an identification with authority which then becomes the absolute value. Buber (4, p. 105) describes the pitfalls of the didactic-inculcating approach:

> I try to explain to my pupils that envy is despicable and at once I feel the secret resistance of those who are poorer than their comrades. I try to explain that it is wicked to bully the weak, and at once I see a suppressed smile on the lips of the strong. I try to explain that lying destroys life, and something frightful happens: the worst habitual liar of the class produces a brilliant essay on the destructive power of lying. I have made the fatal mistake of *giving instructions* in ethics, and what I said is accepted as current coin

of knowledge; nothing of it is transformed into character building substance.

Moral sense cannot be taught or imposed through manipulation and control, or through the use of rewards and punishments. Healthy character evolves through confrontations with others and encounters in the world. When I meet another, when I come up against him, my sense of value must stand as open and clear, as vital and necessary to my being as a moment of sudden insight or self-discovery. In other words, I must be present as a whole person and not permit myself to slip into the role of therapizing or teaching or parenting. I can experience the ethical challenge as an inherent and vital dimension of my world and face this challenge as I might face any issue or problem.

I am speaking of an organic presence, the importance of holding firm on an ethical principle, staying with the moral sense in the same way that one remains with breathing, as a natural and vital process, in the same way that the tree exists which I meet along the path with all its living processes in transaction. The tree simply is there, present, full in being. I relate to it, or not, as its nature and essence register in me. In this sense, the individual can be present in his relations with others, with his spiritual, moral, emotional and intellectual dimensions integrated and unified. Such a person does not instruct, manipulate or control, does not persuade or demand, does not determine values for others; he participates in an ethical or moral realm through sheer presence, through sheer existence. By being an ethical and moral person himself, the person engenders ethical and moral life.

Moral value lies in the *essential* nature of man but its meaning and aliveness emerge as real in the existential moments of experience. In this sense it is beyond essence and beyond existence. It is the source of nourishment and growth but is not itself nourishment or growth.

Is success so important to us as therapists, as educators, as parents, that we are willing to avoid the struggle, the pain, the challenge, the real possibility of loss and failure? Are safety and reward so attractive that we can remain professional or indifferent in the moral realm because to face the issue, to engage in a battle for moral truth involves the danger that the gains, the changes, the successes we value will appear meaningless? Though changes have occurred toward freedom and efficiency in life, are we afraid to recognize that the ultimate unifying theme, the ethical frame, is missing? Do we avoid involvement with another person in the moral realm because at times it is the bitterest struggle of all and threatens our position in the world?

In the moral struggle, the therapist is no longer a therapist, and the teacher is no longer a teacher, and the parent is no longer a parent. The whole person becomes involved from the depths of his being and the struggle is a full human struggle of spirit to spirit. The only reality is the emerging battle and search for the absolute value which alone can give valid meaning to the life being lived, to the reality that exists between two persons, to the encounter in the deepest regions of self to self.

Indifference to value and ethic is a sign of the sickness of man and society. Perhaps this is the most devastating factor of all—indifference to the moral involved; indifference to cruelty and pain; indifference to brutality; indifference to all the moments that register as a significant violation of individual and human rights; indifference to the inner feeling that a wrong direction is being pursued, that a crime against the human dimension is being carried out; indifference to the moral process; indifference to all but one's own status and security; indifference to all but administrative expediency.

Indifference in the moral realm grows out of years of indifference to the deep regions of the self; out of years of conditioning to the system and its routines, procedures, and processes, to rules and doctrines and external signs. The system becomes paramount, ordering behavior and life. At bottom, there is always an ethical and moral value consistent with man's evolution as a human being, a value which can come to life in the concrete, immediate moments of experience.

The absence of value is powerfully illustrated by Yevgeny Yevtushenko in his autobiography. He describes the thousands of Russians crowding into the square to see Stalin's coffin and pay him tribute. Suddenly the mob increases enormously; people are stepped on and crushed. On one side of the square people are blocked by houses, on the other by a row of army trucks. I continue with Yevtushenko's (20, pp. 85-86) description of the ensuing horror:

> "Get those trucks out of the way!" people howled. "Get them out of here!"
>
> "I can't do it! I have no instructions," a very young, towheaded police officer shouted back from one of the trucks, almost crying with helplessness. And people were being hurtled against the trucks by the crowds, and their heads smashed. The sides of the trucks were splashed with blood. All at once I felt a savage hatred for everything that had given birth to that "I have no instructions," shouted at a moment when people were dying because of someone's stupidity. For the first time in my life I thought with hatred of the man we were burying. He could not be innocent of the disaster. It was the "no instructions" that had caused the chaos and bloodshed at his funeral. Now I was certain, once and for all, that you must never wait for instructions if human lives are at stake—you must act. I don't know how I did it, but working energetically with my elbows and fists, I found myself thrusting people aside and shouting "Form chains! Form chains! . . ." And now people understood. They joined hands and formed chains. The strong men and I continued to work at it. The whirlpool was slowing down. The crowd was ceasing to be a savage beast. "Women and children into the trucks!" yelled one of the young men. And women and children, passed from hand to hand, sailed over our heads into the trucks. One of the women who were being handed on was struggling hysterically and whimpering. The young police officer who received her at his end stroked her hair, clumsily trying to calm her down. She shivered a few times and suddenly froze into stillness. The officer took the cap off his straw-colored head, covered her face with it, and burst out crying.

This is entirely the point! We must not live by instructions, by rules, by social, administrative or therapeutic directives but by moral strength, individual and universal value, spiritual strength that can be exercised in the moments of life with other persons when freedom and choice and responsibility are not enough, where there are no instructions but where moral and ethical value provides the directive which gives essence to existence and brings an internal sense which carries its own instructions in the regions of the spirit and the heart and mind of man.

## REFERENCES


1. AQUINAS, ST. THOMAS. *Truth.* Chicago: Henry Regnery Co., 1952.
2. ARISTOTLE. *The Ethics of Aristotle.* Tr. by James A. K. Thomason. Baltimore: Penguin Books, Inc., 1955.
3. BONNER, HUBERT. Idealization and Mental Health. *J. Individ. Psychol.*, Vol. 18, #2, Nov. 1962.
4. BUBER, MARTIN. *Between Man and Man.* Tr. by Ronald G. Smith. London: Routledge & Kegan Paul Ltd., 1947.
5. BUHLER, CHARLOTTE. *Values in Psychotherapy.* New York: Free Press of Glencoe, Division of Macmillan Co., 1962.
6. ECKARDT, MARIANNE H. Self and Identity: A Magic Deception? *Amer. J. Psychoanal.*, Vol. 23, #1, 1963.
7. HARTMAN, ROBERT S. *Individual in Management.* Unpublished paper. Nationwide Management Center, Columbus, Ohio, 1963.
8. KANT, IMMANUEL. *Critique of Pure Reason.* Tr. by F. Max Muller. Garden City, New York: Doubleday and Co., Inc., 1961.
9. KLUCKHOHN, C. Values and Value Orientations in the Theory of Action: An Exploration in Definition and Classification. In T. Parsons and E. A. Shils, Eds., *Toward a General Theory of Action.* Cambridge, Mass.: Harvard University Press, 1952.
10. LEE, DOROTHY. Culture and the Experience of Value. *New Knowledge in Human Values.* A. H. Maslow, Ed. New York: Harper and Bros., 1959.
11. MARGENAU, HENRY. The Scientific Basis of Value Theory. *New Knowledge in Human Values.* A. H. Maslow, Ed. New York, Harper and Bros., 1959.
12. MASLOW, A. H. Further Notes on the Psychology of Being. *J. Humanistic Psychol.*, Vol. 3, #3, Spring, 1963.
13. MASLOW, A. H. Notes on Being Psychology. *J. Humanistic Psychol.*, Vol. 2, #2, Fall, 1962.
14. MOORE, GEORGE E. *Principia Ethica.* Cambridge: Cambridge University Press, 1903.

15. PLATO. *The Republic*. Tr. by B. Jowett. New York: Vintage Books, 1961.
16. PLATO. *Symposium*. Tr. by Percy Bysshe Shelley. Chicago: Henry Regnery Co., 1949.
17. SEWARD, GEORGENE. The Relation Between the Psychoanalytic School and Value Problems in Therapy. *Amer. J. Psychoanal.*, Vol. 22, #2, 1962.
18. SUZUKI, DAISETZ T. Human Values in Zen. *New Knowledge in Human Values*. A. H. Maslow, Ed. New York: Harper and Bros., 1959.
19. TILLICH, PAUL. Is a Science of Human Values Possible? *New Knowledge in Human Values*. A. H. Maslow, Ed. New York: Harper and Bros., 1959.
20. YEVTUSHENKO, YEVGENY. *A Precocious Autobiography*. Tr. by Andrew R. MacAndrew. New York: E. P. Dutton & Co., Inc., 1963.

# 8

# Self-Doubt and Self-Inquiry

Every individual faces the question of the reality and the validity of his own existence. Challenges and unexpected shifts occur in life that arouse and awaken a person to face himself and to doubt the real focus of his world.

To be alive is to be involved with life, and this means being committed. From personal involvement and commitment to life grow affirmative bonds with others. Without commitment, without relatedness, life has no meaning. Yet, inevitably these bonds of relatedness will be threatened and challenged by the uncertain conditions of living, by shattering experiences with others, by disease and death, by any search for perfection and morality in an imperfect and immoral world.

In times of crisis, man questions the meaning of his existence and begins consciously to examine his life. He begins to feel that he is an isolated being existing apart from others, not knowing who he is or where he belongs. In a sense, this doubting of one's own reality is a form of alienation, but alienation is rooted in the human condition.

The process of human life itself, with its unpredictable and complicated changes, often results in inconsistent behavior. Contradictions in the self will occur; sudden shifts in mood, in tempo, in relations, cause one to ponder about life and to become discouraged and disillusioned. Values which appeared to be enduring suddenly deteriorate not only because upheaval is inevitable but because love and certainty, moral consistency, and absolute integrity are ultimately defeated by the sudden shocks of life, by the unpredictable breaks in the pattern of living, and by the restless anxiety man experiences even in a stable existence.

Every person wants to move forward, wants to have new experience, wants to grow. No relationship can remain secure without becoming stagnant and static. Man strives for new directions and new awakenings, and as he does old patterns and bonds are broken, creating a vivid sense of self—sometimes a feeling of victory, sometimes a feeling of defeat and despair.

Dissatisfaction with the security and the repetitious patterns of living and the consequent search for new meaning and new challenge in life is one form of crisis that provokes self-inquiry and self-doubt. This is a central theme in Tolstoi's story *Family Happiness*. I quote several passages from this tale of a crisis in marriage (5, pp. 57-58).

> So two months went by and winter came with its cold and snow; and, in spite of his company, I began to feel lonely, that life was repeating itself, that there was nothing new either in him or myself, and that we were merely going back to what had been before. . . . His unbroken calmness provoked me. I loved him as much as ever and was as happy as ever in his love; but my love, instead of increasing, stood still; and another new and disquieting sensation began to creep into my heart. To love him was not enough for me after the happiness I had felt in falling in love. I wanted movement and not a calm course of existence. . . . I suffered most from the feeling that custom was daily petrifying our lives into one fixed shape, that our minds were losing their freedom and becoming enslaved to the steady passionless course of time. The morning always found us cheerful; we were polite at dinner, and affectionate in the evening. . . . I wanted, not what I had got, but a life of struggle; I wanted feeling to be the guide of life, and not life to guide feeling.

Existential despair often grows out of the demand for self-expression, out of the restless inner spirit that seeks variety and excitement. Dostoevski, reacting against the scientific effort of his time, against attempts to calculate how to achieve the good life, describes man's unpredictable and capricious nature, his refusal to be satisfied with happiness and security (1, pp. 27-28):

> Now I ask you! What can one expect from man since he is a creature endowed with such strange qualities? Shower

> upon him every earthly blessing, drown him in bliss so that nothing but bubbles would dance on the surface of his bliss, as on a sea; give him such economic prosperity that he would have nothing else to do but sleep, eat cakes and busy himself with ensuring the continuation of world history and even then man, out of sheer ingratitude, sheer libel would play you some loathsome trick. . . . It is just his fantastic dreams, his vulgar folly, that he will desire to retain, simply in order to prove to himself (as though that were necessary) that men still are men and not piano keys, which even if played by the laws of nature themselves threaten to be controlled so completely that soon one will be able to desire nothing but by the calendar. . . . I vouch for it, because, after all, the whole work of man seems really to consist in nothing but proving to himself continually that he is a man and not an organ stop.

Dissatisfaction with life is not motivated solely by man's effort to prove that he is not inert, but often grows out of the complex potentialities and forces at work in him and in the universe, existential pressures and demands, and the vicissitudes of life itself. During a human crisis, in moments of self-doubt and self-inquiry, questions naturally arise: "Don't you realize no one really belongs? Don't you know nothing lasts; nothing is permanent?" Just at the moment of rest, when the struggle ends, when a strength of identity has emerged, when a relationship reaches a peak of fullness and beauty, just when we truly experience the glory of existence, life is challenged; it is questioned; it is denied.

Through some sudden event, some crisis, some abrupt change, what a man has known and counted on ceases to be. A pattern of life is broken. Alienation results, not only because man is cut off from what he knows, but also because he questions the reality of his past experience, the reality of what he has perceived and valued and loved. He discovers that a relationship is not as he saw it, that what he regarded as real did not exist. And this shattering insight calls into doubt the reality of his entire life. From such a realization comes despair and disillusion. A search begins, a search for order and harmony in a universe that now appears to be flighty, unstable, and capricious. Disturbance in the sense of self brought about by a sudden break in a significant relationship is expressed in this poem:

I do not know you any more
Once I felt serene in your presence
My heart lifted with the joy of lofty ideals
There was grief and there was laughter
There was beauty in the love of life and nature
The budding leaf, the worn oak tree, mud and water on a
  rainy afternoon, the broken bridge
The wind on the hilltop, the fragrance of warm bread
  and cheese, the walk in the sun, and the moon
Moments of self-fulfillment and love in creation
Experiences varied and real
All that existed between us is no more, instead only
  misty clouds enshroud me
Manacles to restrict a free heart.
Is this also an illusion or have I come to face the truth?
I do not know you any more.

Such shattering breaks in what was believed to be an enduring relationship lead to probing self-inquiry. "Who am I? What do I want? Where do I belong? Where is truth? Where is now? Where is beauty? What is good? What is real?" How still the beat of the night, how sharply ringing the light of day. In such a moment, the restless roaring of the soul envelops man.

I have had many experiences of this kind, experiences in which I entered into my private thoughts in search of meaning, and of self-knowledge. In such moments, human distance is real and the wilderness grows. Across a barren plain a lonely figure waits and searches for a light which is not an illusion, a dream which will not turn out to be fantasy. I want to know that the step I take is real, that my heartbeat is its own, that my ideals will not be meaningless, that love will not be shattered, that my commitment to life will not be broken, that my dreams will not perish. But, how still and silent all is, how barren and meaningless and empty. I hear the mimicry, the mocking voices. I see the critical faces. I go on searching for reality, taking each step with caution, feeling the pain, knowing the horror, experiencing the grief, not giving in but overwhelmed and weakened.

I walk for hours, talking to myself, examining my experience, trying to see within, trying to make sense out of the senselessness and shock. As I walk, as I examine the nature of my life, new questions arise: "What does life mean? Where am I going? Does the way I live really matter?" I look into specific experiences that have been important to me, experiences that have been rich, enjoyable, compelling, in an effort to know what is real, what is genuine, what can be counted on in a world of tragic happenings, of unexpected crises, of disease and death.

My search for an enduring life with others continues. I try to find, within my meetings, one consistent, true, perfect, unchanging relationship. But, as I consider my experiences and meetings, I see dishonesty, deception, cruelty. New and even frightening facets of the self emerge; new faces and sounds appear, faces and voices I do not know, distorted faces and angry, mocking voices. They may exist but for a moment—yet in that moment they cause me to doubt the reality of my perceptions, the substance of my existence, and to search for an ultimate value in life, for an answer to disturbing experiences with the people I know intimately.

A young student suffering from tuberculosis wrote of the pain she experienced in being abandoned by people she thought were real friends, people who forgot her altogether when her hospitalization became prolonged:

> I wonder if it is not better to have no feelings at all. I know now I have lost my friends, whom I thought to be my friends. Some disappeared when they heard about my illness; others after the first months. There are no more tears to shed; nothing can relieve my pain inside of having lost what seemed real and loyal and good. It is as if my heart was being squeezed, little by little, and the droplets keep on falling. I think of the beautiful letter my friend once wrote to me. I thought it was really lovely then. Now I know it was only a piece of paper, a friend of the past easily shattered to bits. Why did this illness happen to me? Why? A thousand times I ask but there is no answer.

Another person speaks of the painful disruption in relations he had always felt to be substantial and enduring:

> I have had to fight a real bitterness; the one way I have been able to do so is to keep silent, not to speak back in anger or revenge; just take a deep sigh, and go on another day, trying to preserve at least a morsel of inner strength and integrity. I seem to be losing so much; yet this doesn't bother me as I have lost so much already, and my one comfort is within. Many have hurt me, even when they tried to help; many so dear to me, in their advice and friendship, heaped so much hurt, until there isn't anything left to hurt.

Each person in his lifetime sees unpleasant faces and hears unpleasant voices. Perhaps one can only continue to be, continue to search for peace and harmony, while at the same time recognizing that life is unpredictable and uncertain. Fame and fortune, sickness and death, failure and defeat, strange inner revolutions and upheavals come unexpectedly, unsolicited, unmotivated, unwarranted.

When resources for self-discovery are exhausted, when a person realizes there is no consistent affirmation in his life with others, he sometimes searches the world of nature for solace. At such moments, I have watched the movement of clouds on dark, foreboding days until the blackness and the heavy rains engulfed me. I have walked in freezing weather until I felt the unrelenting cold everywhere in my body. On a hot summer day, lying quietly, I have waited for the blazing sun to burn through me. I have felt a relatedness to the harsh rain and the bitter cold and the searing heat. I have felt a completeness in the clouds, in the sun, and in the snow. But, soon the rain ceases; the sun departs; and the freezing cold is gone. And once again I am alone searching for the person within myself, the person I can continue to know and continue to be.

At night I have watched the moon until its light radiates through me and, momentarily, I feel I have the answer to my universe, but the moon fades away and the light of our communion disappears. I have walked in the early winter woods searching for growing life. In this silence I find tranquility and beauty. I find peacefulness in being quiet and being alone, but then the blizzard comes and snow covers the forest and the hours of communion in the woods come to an end. A friend expressed the broken tie to nature and the promise of another day in this poem:

Today I was surrounded by the woods.
I walked through them but was not of them.
The woods were busy with their own affairs.
Too busy to greet me whilst I walked in their midst.
Busy with the business of living together.
Each part of the woods,
The roots of the trees intertwined
Both above and below the ground.
The stream gurgled with delight as it met the water
below.
Trees stood together and snow clung to branches.
Only I was alone.
All the sadness of my life crowded upon me.
Nothing to fill the emptiness of my heart.
I turned homeward in the darkening light.
Entering the house, my glance fell on the daffodils.
They greeted me with the freshness of a new wind
And the promise of tomorrow.

Once I walked into a damaged neighborhood. Broken glass and paper littered the streets. Everywhere windows were smashed and the sounds of decay ground in my ears. Yet in this ugliness I stopped to listen to the peaceful singing of the birds. I found a shattered bus collapsed in a vacant field. I entered the bus and remained silent for a long, long time, just sitting, sitting and waiting, experiencing tranquillity within the ruins, feeling completely comfortable and related to the dilapidated place, listening to the quiet chirping of the birds and feeling suddenly at peace with life. One day in a moment of crisis I hurried to this place. Suddenly I felt a strange stirring, an inner warning that something dreadful and very important in my life was imminent. When I reached the vacant lot, the bus was gone. Once again I stood alone in the ruins, in a broken and wasted land.

Then I remembered one dark afternoon when I watched the crackling embers of a fire. As the light began to fade I saw images of a life that was being lived by habit, by routine, a life at the call of others, serving, always serving, a life being lived without full awareness of the meaning and significance of existence. Then suddenly the inner voice was quelled; the light was darkened; the moment was gone.

Who speaks? Who enters the shadow? What does it all mean? So little real knowing! Only in brief times is the full reality, the full human potential lived, only then is the being within its own soaring spirit, encountering life in all its fleeting, changing patterns. There is no I, no me, no knowing of the self, because in a genuine moment all of life is there, as a whole, in harmony, being lived.

To ask the question is itself a search for a new quiet moment, a search for a new birth, a process of exploring in which there is no answer because the solution is within the matrix of existence itself. Such was the experience of a man who sought a new birth in a new relationship by searching into early experiences in his family. Here, he speaks to me:

> I didn't even know if I loved my mother, I didn't even know if I loved my *own* mother. But everybody loves his own mother. You're supposed to love your own mother. Love her? I didn't even know her. That poor soul lying there in the hospital, staring into space, alive, but seeing nothing, was that my mother? The doctor said that it was dementia praecox (what is that?) and it wouldn't be good for me to see her. And then when she was getting worse they said maybe if she saw me it would help. And we rode in the car and she didn't say anything and then she looked at me and said that awful "Norman" with its pleading, questioning, worrying, hopeful, hopeless sound.
>
> And I went back to that private school where I was staying. After class I would go by myself and read the twelve- or thirteen- or God-knows-how-many-volume anthology of the Civil War with its pictures, pictures to stare at. And I stared at them and "Norman," "Norman," "Norman" with that terrible infinite crescendo of a mother's dying dream. But I was only a boy and I couldn't answer, I couldn't answer. I felt the answer inside me but there were no words, only bewilderment. Climb, run, hide, stay where you are. Do something, don't do something, my father, oh, my poor father. And nobody understands and how could I tell my father, tell him what can't be told in words, and these things were always inside me but no words and you just keep them inside and don't know what to do with them.

Then one day you go out and play and you go through the motions of life again. Then you go visit the hospital every other Sunday and you study hard at school and play handball and slowly she gets worse and she's in bed and you argue with your aunt and you do so many petty, mean things. They tell you that you are selfish and that you don't care about others. You worry about the whole world, about starving people and Hitler and you want to do something to save the world; but you are selfish! selfish! selfish!, numbness! numbness! numbness! Nobody feels your feelings and you believe you are selfish, and how can you live with yourself. "You don't care about your father," they say. Inside you feel a deep love for him but he is slipping away from you. And now your mother is flat on her back with that empty, sightless, yet loud pleading stare. You are numb and you feel that there is real physical distance between you and another person, even when you feel his touch. Not psychological distance, but real space. You don't know how you feel, you don't know if you feel. You don't know if you love your mother. You don't know your mother. Did she ever love you? Vague memories of happy times in the park, vague memories of happy feelings, but when and where. Memories of a bad boy, temper tantrums, hurt mother. Did I cause her illness? Someone once said I did. Did I? Did I? Did I?

And the strange times. She hugged me, desperately, desperately hugged me. Why did you hide those things in the refrigerator? But I didn't, I didn't! She sat there rocking, rocking, rocking. She said I had taken money from her pocketbook and she sat there rocking, rocking. Mother please don't rock like that, please, please. And she rocked and rocked. And she hugged me desperately and we were both bewildered and we reached out in despair into the void between us, futility reached out. We were alone, each wanting to engulf the other, and we couldn't touch. Alone and together. . . . Poor father. Poor bewildered father. Poor alone father. Son I'm sorry, and just for a minute we touched. We were together. Together we would help mother. Then aloneness again.

She's dead and it's all over. She's dead. She'd been dead a long time. Who was she? Who in the hell was she! I desperately didn't know, didn't feel. Was I from another planet? Was that why people seemed so strange?

The years went by. Years of numbness and distance. Oh, God, how isolated, how barren is a world in which you can't feel. Time rushes by, with only tiny glimpses into the universe of feeling. It's there but how do you reach it? How? How?"

Yes, in times of tragedy man experiences doubt and despair. He knows the awful feeling of hopelessness and numbness. He realizes the uncertainty, the tentativeness, the provisional nature of human existence.

Again and again the indelible aspects of the universe slip away. Again and again, man realizes there is no final answer to the question "Who am I?" Man engages in self-conscious thought and self-inquiry as a way of identifying himself, or of maintaining his individuality in the face of shocking experience. Inner searching and struggling and suffering will always exist because no part of man's world persists.

During a time of crisis, while trying to hang on to a crumbling world, a friend wrote this letter to me.

> Stand alone sometime soon, very soon, before it is too late, before time has run out; stand alone in the dark night and listen and let yourself be spoken to; listen carefully to what the night has to say; listen carefully to the dark colors upon the ground as they cover up and envelop a tree or rock; listen carefully.
>
> And hear, hear that the night is cold; and ask yourself, when will it be warm; and hear, hear what the cold says; it will be warm soon; very soon. But not an inviting warmth; not a sunny warmth; but a violent warmth, a fiery hell, an inferno of terror, and war; war that has already been seething in the darkness.

The person who is consistently confident and sure, who always knows who he is and where he stands, is reflecting a pattern of routine actions and habits, a self-confident attitude which has grown out of repetition, familiarity, and maintaining the status quo, a refusal to recognize the contradictions which surround him, and a denial of his own restless, searching spirit.

None of us wish to admit that contradictions exist. We come to count on the familiar, stable, ongoing values; we come to depend on routine joy and happiness, on everyday, intimate relationships. We come to depend on those who contribute to our advantage and we give in return, out of a sense of loyalty, duty, and love.

We come to take for granted that each of us will continue to do that which is best for us and for those we love.

Dostoevski has proclaimed that living in such a way, with such reasonable and blissful expectations, is but a golden dream. His conviction is forcefully expressed in the following quotation (1, pp. 18-23):

> Oh, tell me, who first declared, who first proclaimed, that man only does nasty things because he does not know his own real interests; and that if he were enlightened, if his eyes were opened to his real normal interests, man would at once cease to do nasty things, would at once become noble because, being enlightened and understanding his real advantage, he would see his own advantage in the good and nothing else, and we all know that not a single man can knowingly act to his own disadvantage. Consequently, so to say, he would begin doing good through necessity. Oh, the babe! Oh, the pure innocent child! Why, in the first place, when in all these thousands of years has there ever been a time when man has acted only for his own advantage? What is to be done with the millions of facts that bear witness that men, *knowingly*, that is, fully understanding their real advantages, have left them in the background and have rushed headlong on another path, to risk, to chance, compelled to this course by nobody and by nothing, but, as it were, precisely because they did not want the beaten track, and stubbornly, wilfully, went off on another difficult, absurd way seeking it almost in the darkness. . . . Man everywhere and always, whoever he may be, has preferred to act as he wished and not in the least as his reason and advantage dictated. Why, one may choose what is contrary to one's own interests, and sometimes one *positively ought* (that is my idea). One's own free unfettered choice, one's own fancy, however wild it may be, one's own fancy worked up at times to frenzy—why that is that very "most advantageous advantage" which we have overlooked, which comes under no classification and through which all systems and theories are continually being sent to the devil. And how do these sages know that man must necessarily need a rationally advantageous choice? What man needs is simply *independent* choice, whatever that independence may cost and wherever it may lead.

Let a severe crisis come or a calamity, let there be a shock to existence, then the habits and routines give way. Then the person suddenly is aware that he does not know who he is, that many aspects of his life are far from real, far from genuine, that he has slipped into a uniform pattern of living. Let one piece of this apparently stable whole collapse through illness, tragedy, false encounters, the discovery of truth, death, or the awful awareness of finitude or imperfection, and a shocking awakening takes place. Let this awareness break through to the surface and intense anguish is aroused and a desperate search for a genuine life is undertaken. Such a shattering awakening brings with it a thousand questions, the competing and opposing strands of life, the competing and opposing wishes and wills, the realization that in no single meeting is there permanence, or absolute morality; in no single relationship can one maintain perfect ethics, pure and consistent humanistic principles. The shattering of a self-image brings with it not only self-doubt and inner disturbance but a doubting of the reality of all of life. Such a crisis was faced by Ivan Ilych, Tolstoi's protagonist, who thought he had really lived until the day of his sudden, impending death. Ivan struggled painfully with questions of life and death, of truth and reality, of uniformity and individuality, of meaning and absurdity, of grief and unjust suffering. He searched deeply into his life, as the following passages attest (4, pp. 146-156):

> "Why hast Thou done all this? Why hast Thou brought me here? Why, why dost Thou torment me so terribly?"
>
> He did not expect an answer and yet wept because there was no answer and could be none. The pain again grew more acute, but he did not stir and did not call. He said to himself: "Go on! Strike me! But what is it for? What have I done to Thee? What is it for?"
>
> Then he grew quiet and not only ceased weeping but even held his breath and became all attention. It was as though he were listening not to an audible voice but to the voice of his soul, to the current of thoughts arising within him.
>
> "What is it you want?" was the first clear conception capable of expression in words, that he heard.
>
> "What do you want? What do you want?" he repeated to himself.
>
> "What do I want? To live and not to suffer," he answered.

And again he listened with such concentrated attention that even his pain did not distract him.

"To live? How?" asked his inner voice.

"Why, to live as I used to—well and pleasantly."

"As you lived before, well and pleasantly?" the voice repeated.

And in imagination he began to recall the best moments of his pleasant life. But strange to say none of those best moments of his pleasant life now seemed at all what they had then seemed—none of them except the first recollections of childhood. There, in childhood, there had been something really pleasant with which it would be possible to live if it could return. But the child who experienced that happiness existed no longer, it was like a reminiscence of somebody else.

As soon as the period began which had produced the present Ivan Ilych, all that had then seemed joy now melted before his sight and turned into something trivial and often nasty. . . . His marriage, a mere accident, then the disenchantment that followed it, his wife's bad breath and the sensuality and hypocrisy: then that deadly official life and those preoccupations about money, a year of it, and two, and ten, and twenty, and always the same thing. And the longer it lasted the more deadly it became. "It is as if I had been going downhill while I imagined I was going up. And that is really what it was. I was going up in public opinion, but to the same extent life was ebbing away from me. And now it is all done and there is only death."

"Then what does it mean? It can't be that life is so senseless and horrible. But if it really has been so horrible and senseless, why must I die and die in agony? There is something wrong!"

"Maybe I did not live as I ought to have done," it suddenly occurred to him. "But how could that be, when I did everything properly?" he replied, and immediately dismissed from his mind this, the sole solution of all the riddles of life and death, as something quite impossible.

"Then what do you want now? To live? Live how? Live as you lived in the law courts when the usher proclaimed "The judge is coming!" "The judge is coming, the judge!" he repeated to himself. "Here he is, the judge. But I am not guilty!" he exclaimed angrily. "What is it for?" . . .

"Resistance is impossible!" he said to himself. "If I could only understand what it is all for! But that too is impossible. An explanation would be possible if it could be said that I have not lived as I ought to. But it is impossible to say that," and he remembered all the legality, correctitude, and propriety of his life. "That at any rate can certainly not be admitted," he thought, and his lips smiled ironically as if someone could see that smile and be taken in by it. "There is no explanation! Agony, death . . . What for?"

The question suddenly occurred to him: "What if my whole life has really been wrong?"

It occurred to him that what had appeared perfectly impossible before, namely that he had not spent his life as he should have done, might after all be true. It occurred to him that his scarcely perceptible attempts to struggle against what was considered good by the most highly placed people, those scarcely noticeable impulses which he had immediately suppressed, might have been the real thing, and all the rest false. And his professional duties and the whole arrangement of his life and of his family, and all his social and official interests, might all have been false. He tried to defend all those things to himself and suddenly felt the weakness of what he was defending. There was nothing to defend.

"But if that is so," he said to himself, "and I am leaving this life with the consciousness that I have lost all that was given me and it is impossible to rectify it—what then?"

For three whole days, during which time did not exist for him, he struggled in that black sack into which he was being thrust by an invisible, resistless force. He struggled as a man condemned to death struggles in the hands of the executioner, knowing that he cannot save himself. And every moment he felt that despite all his efforts he was drawing nearer and nearer to what terrified him. He felt that his agony was due to his being thrust into that black hole and still more to his not being able to get right into it. He was hindered from getting into it by his conviction that his life had been a good one. That very justification of his life held him fast and prevented his moving forward, and it caused him most torment of all.

Suddenly some force struck him in the chest and side, making it still harder to breathe, and he fell through the hole and there at the bottom was a light. What had happened to him was like the sensation one sometimes experiences in a railway carriage when one thinks one is going backwards while one is really going forwards and suddenly becomes aware of the real direction.

"Yes, it was all not the right thing," he said to himself, "but that's no matter. It can be done. But what is the right thing?" he asked himself, and suddenly grew quiet.

This occurred at the end of the third day, two hours before his death. Just then his schoolboy son had crept softly in and gone up to the bedside. The dying man was still screaming desperately and waving his arms. His hand fell on the boy's head, and the boy caught it, pressed it to his lips, and began to cry.

At that very moment Ivan Ilych fell through and caught sight of the light, and it was revealed to him that though his life had not been what it should have been, this could still be rectified. He asked himself, "What is the right thing?" and grew still, listening.

And suddenly, it grew clear to him what had been oppressing him and would not leave him was all dropping away at once from two sides, and ten sides, and from all sides. He was sorry for them, he must act so as not to hurt them: release them and free himself from these sufferings.

"What has become of it? Where are you, pain?"

He turned his attention to it.

"Yes, here it is. Well, what of it? Let the pain be."

"And death . . . where is it?"

He sought his former accustomed fear of death and did not find it. Where is it? What death? There was no fear because there was no death.

In place of death there was light.

The crisis of a dying man in touch with himself is that even if his life has not been worthwhile, he must in the end find meaning and value. He may see that he has lived falsely. In his search and struggle for meaning and justification for living, there often is only the echo of footsteps and the slow and heavy beat of the heart.

During critical moments of self-inquiry, I am not I, yet *not* not I either. I am apart, walking in the sunlight, seeing the pieces of a broken cast. I enter them. I hear the whining, complaining voices around me; now they are unreal. I speak from the depths of my soul; no one listens. It is a moment beyond all other moments and it contains a truth which has not existed before. Around me the hurried pace continues, the rugged knock, the impressive face, the shallow embrace, how lucky we all are! The breath I take is a solitary breath amidst the silence of the broken cast, tossed aside. But I am here. I exist. I am real even if for only a moment. There is stillness now and in that stillness there is a struggle for the dawn, a struggle for a new life of truth and beauty and goodness, a struggle to accept reality. This is the message of a friend who in the last weeks of terminal cancer questioned the meaning of life:

> Yes, this is a new beginning
> For I who died, am alive again today,
> And this is the eve of the moon's fullness.
>
> This is a new beginning
> For I who died, find strength to live today,
> Remembering the pleasures of meetings real.
>
> This is a new beginning
> For I who died alone, arise to find
> That life is aloneness and cannot be possessed.
>
> This is a new beginning
> For I who died now know, the moon and life are there,
> For each to love and share.

Self-inquiry is a painful process in which life is viewed with a new perception, a new awareness. What was accepted, as a matter of course, now comes into doubt. Is it real? What does it mean? Was this relationship, this situation, ever genuine? What kind of game have I been playing? The old perceptions no longer hold. Each detail is considered from the perspective of a new self searching for a new identity. At such a time, man becomes conscious, aware, painfully sensitive. The world can never be the same again. The scenes of life which had passed unnoticed now become sharply real. Their meaning, their value, their genuineness, must be considered from the pointed perspective of a new, emerging self. In such moments, man realizes the importance of being real, of being fully honest, of maintaining his individuality. All else becomes secondary. The little remarks, the sidelong glances, the probings and pushings, become painful references, and the struggle continues: "Who am I?" "What do I really want?" "What is the meaning of it all?" "Where do I belong?"

But there is no immediate answer, not within one's self, not in one's relations with other persons, and not in the universe of nature and inanimate life. Neither love nor comradeship can quiet this anguished self searching for a lasting reality. Nor can they temper the painful rawness of a self in search of authenticity, in search of permanence and continuity, a self which reaches exhaustive peaks of inquiry followed by moments of the quiet evenness of isolation. Who asks? Who speaks? Who enters the shadow and the light? There is no final word, only the question, only the revolution of a self confronting the reality of life and the apparent absurdity of existence. The process of self-inquiry which follows the human crisis brings with it certain searing questions.

What is life? Where are the stars and the moon? What is left to mar? Is there no lasting love with love? No answer to the conflict, no indelible way to live? Where is man to be infinitely affirmed? In the stones, in the woods, in the soil? Must life forever be less than whole? Why is it not permanently good and noble as it is meant to be?

The process of self-doubt initiated by a shock to existence must run its course, must reach its own level before one can live again in the reality of not knowing, in the senseless anxieties of contemporary life, and in the emptiness and meaninglessness of daily habit and routines of work, rest, and play. Then the question of the meaning of life is not asked, not because one knows the answer, but because one no longer need ask.

Man returns to living and arrives at the conviction that love is real and that life has a rich, enduring meaning. Even in the darkest hours man will search for confirmation of the ideal because he wants to believe that human values are enduring. Though human value and love will inevitably be challenged and defeated and crushed, man will resurrect them because he can never completely eradicate his belief in universal ties, his belief that all living beings and forms contain a unique identity and a sense of permanency. Though defeat is inevitable, hope and faith are eternal.

Life continues on but not in the same way. The struggle has not been a waste. Though there is no permanent answer to the fragile nature and absurdity of existence, the search for meaning leads to real moments of experience. When the inquiry is over, a vision returns, the brevity of time and a desire for permanence in being and in relation, and with it the knowledge that the vision of permanence can never be realized. In the final words of MacLeish's play, *J. B.* (3):

> We can never *know* . . .
> He answered me like the . . .
>                                 stillness of a star
> That silences us, asking.
> We *are* and that is all our answer.
> We are and what we are can suffer . . .
> But . . .
>         what suffers, loves . . .
>                                 and love
> Will live its suffering again,
> Risk its own defeat again,
> Endure the loss of everything again
> And yet again and yet again
> In doubt, in dread, in ignorance, unanswered,
> Over and over, with the dark before,
> The dark behind it . . .
>                         and still live . . .
>                                 still love.

Questions of self-doubt and self-inquiry are not signs of sickness or collapse. The fact that so many persons involved in the struggle to live decently and meaningfully are asking, "Who am I?" registers emphatically man's response to the existential paradox, to the inevitable conditions of change and upheaval. Viktor Frankl puts it thus (2, p. 12):

> I do not want to give the impression that the existential vacuum in itself represents a mental disease: the doubt whether one's life has a meaning is an existential despair, it is a spiritual distress rather than a mental disease. . . . The search for a meaning to one's existence, even the doubt whether such a meaning can be found at all, is something human and nothing morbid.

Man seeks consistency. He strives for perfection, knowledge, awareness. He wants a permanent union with his fellow man, with God, with the universe. But there is no absolute consistency; there is no perfection. Uncertainty, insecurity, temporality, finitude, restlessness, new awakenings, are the ultimate realities of human existence.

No, to ask the question, to inquire into life, to doubt the sensibility of existence, these are not questions of a disturbed and thwarted mind. These are questions which man will always ask, in sickness and in health, because they are rooted in the organic pattern of life itself. And because man strives for the infinite, man will forever be frustrated and discouraged, forever doomed to suffer. But in the suffering, in the struggle, he achieves his individuality and his identity. When there is a striking failure in life, man will always return to himself. For ultimately man is alone.

In the Upanishads there is a story about Yajnavalkya, the sage at the king's court. The king asked him one day, "By what light do human beings go out, do their work and return?" The sage answered, "By the light of the sun." The king then asked, "But when the light of the sun is extinguished, by what light do human beings go out, do their work and return?" The sage said, "By the light of the moon." And so question and answer went on. When the moon is extinguished, man works by the light of the stars; when they are quenched, by the light of the fire. And when the light of the fire itself is put out, the king asked, "By what light then can they do their work and still live?" The sage replied: "By the light of the self."

Though such a search for permanent answers is bound to be futile, it is a necessary step to creation, to rebirth, to renewal. For man will return to live again, believing in the fundamental goodness of life. Not knowing who he is or where he belongs, he will find love again and this will provide, if only temporarily, a pervasive meaning to his life.

In times of self-doubt and despair all of life appears unreal, false, dishonest, even brutal. Then one day you find someone who listens, who loves, someone gentle who feels your presence and you start gradually to exist again, to feel, to trust, to be a genuine person. You begin to believe in life and to live, without rancor or fear, in the midst of joy and beauty and friendship. The tragedy is over and you have been born anew. Life takes on a sense of permanency. In the midst of this passion for life, there is a continuing sense of self-realizing. Now life is infinite; it is honorable; it is worthwhile. The meaning of life is no longer questioned. In such times, man no longer seeks an answer to the riddle, "Who am I?" He does not probe into his relationships. He does not inquire into the meaning of life. He exists and that is all that matters. He experiences not doubt and suspicion, not tentativeness and uncertainty, but the four great stages of man so beautifully illustrated by Van der Post in *The Heart of the Hunter* (6, pp. 253-266). He feels that life has a meaning only in living, only through creations beyond the immediate self; he realizes that acts of creation must emerge in the context of a community on earth; he believes that life being lived in a community must be lived as an individual, and he sees that man must renew himself by renewing his relationship with God, with the universe, with divine life, beyond the individual and beyond the community.

In the end, out of the broken chain of life circumstances, man chooses to live again, however shocking is the perfidy that surrounds him. By choosing to live again he makes a commitment to life. This commitment reflects the essential belief and faith in human beings, a conviction that man's relation to himself, to others and to the universe is dependable and trustworthy. Transcending the tragedy of the human condition, man finds again a belief in his own capacity to live authentically, a belief in the enduring values of faith and love, not only for himself but for humanity and for all that exists in the world and beyond it.

## REFERENCES

1. DOSTOEVSKI, FYODOR. *Notes From Underground and The Grand Inquisitor*. Tr. by Ralph Matlaw. New York: E. P. Dutton & Co., Inc., 1960.
2. FRANKL, VIKTOR. Dynamics, Existence, and Values. *J. of Existential Psychiat.*, Vol. 2, 5-16, Summer, 1961.
3. MACLEISH, ARCHIBALD. *J. B.* R.C.A. Records. Elia Kazan Producer.
4. TOLSTOI, LEO. The Death of Ivan Ilych in *Quintet*. New York: Medalion Publishing Corp., 1956.

5. TOLSTOI, LEO. Family Happiness in *The Death of Ivan Ilych and Other Stories*. New York: The New American Library of World Literature, Inc., 1960.
6. VAN DER POST, LAURENS. *The Heart of the Hunter*. New York: William Morrow and Co., 1961.

# 9

## Dimensions of the Creative Life

Every person has within himself the potentiality for creative living, for participating in interhuman experience on an authentic basis while maintaining a distinctive and unique individuality. Yet, in spite of this inherent capacity, men have turned away from each other, away from human meaning and integrative expressions of a genuine self. Increasingly, they have turned toward a safe and standard way of life, toward the routine monotony of repetitive activities, surface expressions, and conventional relationships. Most meetings have come to be conforming interactions between ghosts of people rather than exciting, fundamental relationships. Most meetings are based on intellectual habits and external guides, on the values of the system or, as Ken Kesey calls it, "the combine," rather than on values of the self.

When people are genuinely related they create for themselves and for each other new feelings, new experiences, a new life. They learn to trust the mystery and wonder in themselves and in the world, and thus take the journey into an expanding self-awareness and an enlarging reality. But when a person says something that is appraised and adjusted, reacted to and balanced off, when he speaks in order to put his idea in "proper perspective" and to compete for status, then he is no longer present as an integrated human being. He is reacting, participating as a reactor, in response to an external event. He is not a spontaneous person, involved in real living. Talking is the object of talk, and the flow of words prevents the experiencing of anxiety that should be felt from meaningless and empty conversation.

Unfortunately, modern society does not encourage

diversity and individuality, does not center in genuine interhuman experience between real persons. Ambitious parents may set up goals and communicate expectations indirectly and deviously (so that what they really want and expect from the child registers clearly at subliminal levels regardless of what they actually say). Or, quite openly, parents may program the child's life in such a way that he progresses step by step toward their values, their goals, their expected achievements.

Often the individual is unaware that he, as a unique growing person, has been cancelled out and in place of his genuine self there is only a concept, a definition of what he should be—and that definition so pieced together that the individual lacks substance and identity. The living qualities of sensitivity and awareness remain hidden, dwarfed, and undeveloped.

The self is not its concept any more than a tree (or any other living thing) is its definition. The parts pieced together do not make an integrated whole. They are fragments of a self which can achieve unity only through expression of real feelings, real desires, real interests, and self-values. The mode or average, regardless of theories of numbers and mechanics, can only have relevance as a statistical construct. It is not the living stuff, the ideal, or even the healthy path for men to take. For all its safety and comfort, the golden mean is still only a fictitious and mechanical number. It exists in fantasy, although that fantasy may be more real for "average" persons that reality itself.

Unfortunately, the "average," does not remain in tables and charts and textbooks, but finds its way into the schools and into the dead process of modern education. In modern schools the activities are often mechanical and unimaginative, and the already alienated child is grouped and lesson-planned so that he takes one more step into exile, moves farther and farther away from his own unique selfhood. At last he becomes convinced that he is average and that his averageness is all there is to him. He rejects the one dimension of himself that can still bring meaning to his existence—his own yes-feeling.

The values and resources that exist within the deep regions of himself have not been tapped and explored, and so he becomes one of the sea of faces, one of the modulated and patterned voices. Along with the subject matter, *he* becomes programmed. Often his uniqueness in the world is not even noticed. Anxious to play his part and please, indifference does not matter in the least.

He got that way in the first place because he was not valued and confirmed as a self. His parents did not take their cues from him, did not love him as an independent self with his own strange and peculiar avenues of expression. They did not help him to open up new regions, to explore new territories that would get their initial value from him, from the movements of his body, from his growing awareness of life, and from his wish to explore life on his own terms.

Thus he begins to take his cues from the outside, learning to do that which is proper, that which is approved. He learns to be motivated by the right incentives and the right rewards, to adjust to external circumstances, to play the game, to carry out his role. And in the process, he denies his own unique heritage and his destiny as a particular person. To him adjustment becomes the goal of life. Successful adjustment may, of course, be advantageous in offering superficial happiness in the form of materialistic and social benefits. But at the same time it reduces individuals to collective modes, to the least common denominator, to a mechanical way of life that lacks ethical and moral commitment, preventing the realization of higher ideals, and repressing the imaginative, daring, and creative ventures that characterize the spontaneous living of unique persons. Yet underneath, real feelings, real interests, real talents, not entirely stifled, are pressing for expression and fulfillment.

Motivation is often used to trap attention and coerce effort, to persuade people to engage in projects which have no intrinsic worth. Tensions are developed within the individual which must then be resolved through achievement and activity. Strivings for equilibrium, release of tensions, and death wishes are erroneous representations of healthy life. The tendency to seek and maintain an existent or "safe" state is characteristic of sick people, a sign of anomaly and decay (2). In the healthy person, autonomy, spontaneity, and self-direction are the guiding forces in the development of unique identity and creative life. Motivating a person to adjust is an external means of influencing which leads to inauthentic, conformist living. Adjustment is not a positive assertion of the self. It does not indicate who a man is and what he is living for, but is a form of giving in to external pressures.

The alienated individual experiences a constant vague sense of anxiety. Life is brief, time passes, and the authentic sources of being are drying up. More and more the limit of time becomes a threatening realization, and a sense of incompleteness and despair often overwhelms the person. This is the despair of self-abrogation and self-denial. Kierkegaard in terse, moving expressions describes the despair of self-denial in his book, *The Sickness Unto Death* (4, pp. 342-344).

> A despairing man is in despair over something. So it seems for an instant, but only for an instant, that same instant the true despair manifests itself, or despair manifests itself in its true character. For in the fact that he despaired of something, he really despaired of himself, and now would be rid of himself. Thus when the ambitious man whose watchword was "Either Caesar or nothing" does not become Caesar, he is in despair thereat. But this signifies something else, namely, that precisely because he did not become Caesar he now cannot endure to be himself . . . In a profounder sense it is not the fact that he did not become Caesar which is intolerable but the self which did not become Caesar is the thing that is intolerable; or, more correctly, what is intolerable to him is that he cannot get rid of himself. . . .

Three methods or attitudes of modern living contribute to the deterioration of uniqueness and individuality and the development of mass behavior and mass identity: analysis, diagnosis, and evaluation. By such approaches we seek and find the weaknesses and inadequacies, the abnormalities and deviations in ourselves and others. We set up norms, establish categories, and create hierarchies that close the doors of perception and predispose individuals to look for and find in themselves and in the world the objects and fragments of "good" living rather than the good life itself. We create classes, castes, and divisions that separate the individual from his own spontaneous inclinations, resources, and values and divide man from man. We create categorical distinctions and competitive strivings for victory and glory. Sometimes we think that through diagnosis, analysis and evaluation we can find the hidden pieces of a puzzle and put them together to form an insightful picture, but such a scheme is effective only in a closed system. Man is not bounded by a fence or frame. He is open to new emerging life and at any moment he can cast the picture puzzle to the winds and make a choice that alters the entire nature of his existence.

We can never find our real selves or any other person through diagnosis, evaluation, or analysis. These methods break up the self and attempt to objectify and make finite what is essentially personal, unified, and infinite. They are inevitably fixed in the past and fail to recognize the emerging powers of choice, promise, and the sudden new awarenesses and discoveries and creations of a unique growing person. Inevitably analysis is a destructive approach, looking as it does behind reality for causes and events instead of recognizing that reality is contained in the immediate experiences of the person and in his unfolding life. Progoff (6, p. 60) affirms this position in the following statement:

> When the person becomes self-consciously analytical, the momentum of growth is lost. This is so for several reasons, any one of which can permanently stunt the process of creative development. One reason is that when the person begins to think of himself in the light of pathology his image grows dim. The thoughts he projects are thoughts of weakness and they refer to the difficulties experienced along the road of development rather than to the unfolding essence of the process as a whole. When they are described and diagnosed and are given the respectability of pathologic forms, they become entities with a reality of their own. The focus of attention is then placed upon the transient pathology of the process and the energy latent in the seed of potentiality is not drawn upon.

Analytical knowledge, despite all its content of "truth," remains fragmentary and limited. A life based on this kind of knowledge does not flow from the spontaneous, creative powers of the self but from external signs and directions. Even the person with severe emotional problems does not need diagnosis and analysis. What he requires is genuine human experience, meetings with real persons. Then his capacity for living and experiencing may still be able to save him.

A science that objectifies, evaluates, and puts people in categories eliminates the real persons. It sets up impersonal and unalterable standards and categories based on fragmented views of behavior. It deals with elements of sameness. Such a science abstracts until eventually persons and things become nothing at all. For example, a flower is nothing when we analyze it and abstract its characteristics and qualities, but it is positively a flower when we enjoy it in absorption with nature. The reality of experience and the personal creations of the individual can never be known in analysis and abstraction, can never be known by precise measurement, but only through a meaningful integration of immediate experience. The unique and idiosyncratic qualities of experience cannot be observed, defined, and classified but must *be lived to be really known.* John Steinbeck and Edward F. Ricketts (8) express this view in the following passage:

> We knew that what we could see and record and construct would be warped, as all knowledge patterns are warped, first, by the collective pressure and stream of our time and race, second by the thrust of our individual personalities. But knowing this, we might not fall into too many holes—we might maintain some balance between our warp and the separate thing, the external reality. The oneness of these two might take its contribution from both. For example: the Mexican sierra has XVII-15IX spines in the dorsal fin. These can easily be counted. But if the fish sounds and nearly escapes and finally comes in over the rail, his colors pulsing and his tail beating the air, a whole new relational externality has come into being—an entity which is more than the sum of the fish plus the fisherman. The only way to count the spines of the sierra unaffected by this second relational reality is to sit in a laboratory, open an evil-smelling jar, remove a stiff colorless fish from formalin solution, count the spines, and write the truth D.XVII-15IX. There you have recorded a reality which cannot be assailed, probably the least important reality concerning either the fish or yourself.

> It is good to know what you are doing. The man with his pickled fish has set down one truth and has recorded in his experience many lies. The fish is not that color, that texture, that dead, nor does it smell that way.

The creative life always involves an integrative concern with life as a whole, in which understanding emerges from growing experiences, based on ethical and moral value and not on analysis and evaluation. The creative life is always based on self-values, not on the values of the system.

Creative living involves meetings between real persons in which each expresses himself, not within a prescribed role, not as an expert, not in accordance with rules and conventions, but as a person with unified skills and talents, a person who lives wholly within the requirements of each situation. The result of such experience may be the emergence of an enlightened and open person, or the return to health of an emotionally sick one. But such change is the natural outcome of important human experiences. It is not something to be sought for, but something that happens.

## INTRINSIC NATURE, BEING, BECOMING

Three central, orienting concepts of self are: intrinsic nature, being, and becoming. Intrinsic nature refers to the natural, inherent, given, unchanging potentialities, or proclivities of man, whose interest it is to realize these inherent potentialities, to develop himself as fully and completely as possible. Inner nature is universally noncomparable, absolute, inviolate. Its focus, orientation, and unity in any one individual is always unique.

There is no such things as *a type* of person (except for "useful" abstracting purposes). The experience of one's separateness as a human being represents both the necessity and the opportunity for the person to manifest basic tendencies, to develop a personality. The continuing creation of man's uniqueness is guided by values, based upon the unconscious or pre-conscious perceptions of our own nature, of our own "call" in life.

The harmony and emergence of one's own life seem to

come from the increasing capacity to find in the world that which also obtains within the depths of one's own being. The self emerges in appropriate patterns of experience that incorporate the inherent truth of the organism. Being refers to this concrete, holistic patterning of self in immediate living, as well as the unyielding, absolute, and unique qualities of the individual person. The individual self, or being, is an ultimate core of reality which remains unchanged throughout changes of its qualities or states. To be, a person must be true to himself and his inner nature, in real experience. The sources for the assertion of human potentialities are deep within the personal experiences of the one who asserts them. And one can discover his real self only as an autonomous entity. Being is good only as itself and can be understood as a whole only in itself alone—not in terms of its attributes. It is an indivisible unity.

True experience is the natural expression of one's inner self in interaction with people and resources. As such, all expressions in true experience are creative. True experience involves an immanent orientation characterized by the immediate knowing of the world through direct, personal perception. All the significant undertakings of our past lives are embedded in our present selves and cannot be isolated without violating the essence of experience.

The individual is engaged in leading his life in the present, with a forward thrust in the future. This is the concept of becoming, with its implications of change and transformation. Creation is conceived as a continual transition from one form to another. The world, while it is being perceived, is being incessantly created by an individual who is a process, not a product. The individual is not a fixed entity but a center of experience involving the creative synthesis of relations. The central force for this becoming nature of man is a basic striving to assert and expand his self-determination, to create his own fate.

The organism has different potentialities. And because it has them, it has the need to realize them. The fulfillment of these needs represents the self-actualization of the organism, the constant emerging of self, of one's "nature" in the world. Failure to actualize essential capacities is equivalent to not being. Every individual wants to become himself. All reality is this process of becoming. All life is one, a constant urge to become.

According to his intrinsic nature, the individual develops certain appropriate needs, sensitivities, inhibitions, and moral values. If he can grow in love and in friction, he will also grow in accordance with his real self. To the extent that painful experiences foster and fulfill our inner nature, they are desirable experiences. Growth in self-fulfilling persons can come through struggle, agony, and conflict, as well as through tranquility, joy, and love—or through any other emotion.

## UNITY AND SELF-CONSISTENCY

Personal growth as portrayed here stresses the unity and organization of man. Personality is conceived as an organization of values which are consistent with one another. In all personal transformations, certain persistent and distinguishable characteristics and values remain.

In a real sense there is one whole, the totality of being. To view the person in parts or pieces is not only invalid but a denial of the integrity and respect entitled to every human being, a denial of his right to be regarded as himself, as a whole person. Segmented behavior is an expression of the individual's effort to remove a condition which interferes with unity and self-actualization.

The real person responds entirely, wholly. He organizes and unifies his perceptions of his immediate personal world so as to have value and meaning appropriate to his personality. The life of the individual is an organized patterned process, a distinctiveness of pattern which constitutes both the unity and distinctiveness of self. All past processes obtain their specific function from the unifying over-all pattern of the individual. The necessity to maintain this unity of the self is a universal dynamic principle.

How does a person know if he is truly himself, if he is growing in terms of his unique potentialities, if he is developing his own special human resources? There is no objective way of knowing, no external evidence by which these questions can be answered. Only through subjective, inner experiences and convictions, in moments of solitude, can one come to feel the authenticity of being.

A letter writen by the poet Rilke (7, pp. 17-22) in answer to a young writer who sought his advice, beautifully expresses the importance of inner searching and conviction. I present it below, with some omissions.

> You ask whether your verses are good. You ask me. You have asked others before. You send them to magazines. You compare them with other poems, and you are disturbed when certain editors reject your efforts. Now (since you have allowed me to advise you) I beg you to give up all that. You are looking outward, and that above all you should not do now. Nobody can counsel and help you, that bids you write; find out whether it is spreading out its roots in the deepest places of your heart, acknowledge to yourself whether you would have to die if it were denied you to write. This above all—ask yourself in the stillest hour of your night: must I write: Delve into yourself for a deep answer. And if this should be affirmative, if you may meet this earnest question with a strong and simple "I must," then build your life according to this necessity; your life even into its most indifferent and slightest hour must be a sign of this urge and a testimony to it . . . And if out of this turning inward, out of this absorption into your own world verses come, then it will not occur to you to ask anyone whether they are good verses. . . . for you will see in them your fond natural possession, a fragment and a voice of your life. A work of art is good if it has sprung from necessity. In this nature of its origin lies the judgment of it: there is no other. Therefore, my dear sir, I know no advice for you save this: go into yourself and test the deeps in which your life takes rise; at its source you will find the answer to the question whether you must create. Accept it, just as it sounds without inquiring into it. Perhaps it will turn out that you are called to be an artist. Then take that destiny upon yourself and bear it, its burden and its greatness, without ever asking what recompense might come from outside. For the creator must be a world for himself and find everything in himself and in Nature to whom he has attached himself. . . .

The truly human relationship is an encounter in which two persons meet simply and openly in a spirit of unity. In such a relationship nothing intervenes—no system of ideas, no foreknowledge, no aims, not even anticipations. It is a matter of being, of presence, of life being lived, rather than a matter of individuals acting and being acted upon.

Sometimes it is necessary for one person to help another gain courage and strength to act on his own. A famous passage from Plato's Seventh Letter emphasizes this point: "After much converse about the matter itself and a life lived together, suddenly a light as it were, is kindled in one soul by a flame that leaps to it from another, and thereafter sustains itself. . . ."

It is truly a matter of touching something within a person, bringing into activity a potential already present, or an actuality temporarily blocked or stifled. It means freeing the other person to recover his own nature, to express himself, and to discover his capacities. Every act of helping another to fulfill his unique potentialities is at the same time an actualization of one's own capacity for self-growth. It is the realization of the capacity for meeting a person as a person and valuing him as he is.

In the creative relationship, changes occur not because one person deliberately sets out to influence and alter the behavior or attitude of another person but because it is inevitable that when individuals really meet as persons and live together in a fundamental sense they will modify their behavior so that it is consistent with values and ideals which lead to self-realizing ends. The creative relationship is an experience of mutual involvement, commitment, and participation, a meeting of real persons. It can be studied or learned in a static and discrete sense, but it can be known only through living.

The life of any person or thing is its own. All that man can do is affect the environment in which potentialities can be fulfilled. Materials and resources can be provided which may enrich experience, but in real growth the individual alone determines his direction and his reality. Tenderness, care, personal warmth, confirmation, all affect the development of the individual and the enhancement of the self.

It is within the power of man to treasure his personality, to strengthen and value his individuality; to turn toward honesty, affection, self-respect; toward intellectual and aesthetic growth; and to turn away from destructive analysis, self-degradation, alienation, hypocrisy, cruelty, cowardliness, and smallness.

## CONCLUDING COMMENT

In the creative human relationship there is a feeling that soars beyond the limits of self-awareness and into the heart of another person. There is a feeling of oneness, a feeling of communion. There is the freedom of being that enables each person to be spontaneous and responsible. Freedom means opening oneself to a relationship, experiencing it as positive and unique. It means allowing whatever will happen to happen, not forcing the direction or the results. It means expressing one's talents and skills immediately, spontaneously, and in accordance with the unique requirements of each human situation.

## REFERENCES


1. BUBER, MARTIN. *I and Thou.* Translated by Ronald G. Smith. New York: Charles Scribner's Sons, 1937.
2. GOLDSTEIN, KURT. *The Organism.* New York: American Book Co., 1939.
3. KESEY, KEN. *One Flew Over the Cuckoo's Nest.* New York: Viking Press, Inc., 1962.
4. KIERKEGAARD, SÖREN. *A Kierkegaard Anthology.* Edited by Robert Bretall. Princeton, New Jersey: Princeton University Press, 1951.
5. MOUSTAKAS, CLARK, Ed. *The Self: Explorations in Personal Growth.* New York: Harper and Row, 1956.
6. PROGOFF, IRA. *The Symbolic and The Real.* New York: Julian Press, Inc., 1963.
7. RILKE, RAINER MARIA. *Letters to a Young Poet.* Translated by M. D. Herter Norton. Rev. ed. New York: W. W. Norton & Co., Inc., 1954.
8. STEINBECK, JOHN and RICKETTS, EDWARD F. *Sea of Cortez.* New York: Viking Press, Inc., 1941.

# Index